AN
ECLIPSE
of the SOUL

AN ECLIPSE

of the SOUL

A Christian Resource
on Dealing with Suicide

Helen Kooiman Hosier

Revell
Grand Rapids, Michigan

© 1974, 1978, 2005 by Helen Kooiman Hosier

Published by Fleming H. Revell
a division of Baker Publishing Group
P.O. Box 6287, Grand Rapids, MI 49516-6287

Previously published in 1974 under the title *Going Sideways: Hope, Love, Life versus Suicide* by Hawthorn Books and in 1978 under the title *Suicide, a Cry for Help* by Harvest House Publishers.

Printed in the United States of America

Library of Congress Cataloging-in-Publication Data
Hosier, Helen Kooiman.
    An eclipse of the soul : a Christian resource on dealing with suicide / Helen Kooiman Hosier.
        p.   cm.
    Revised ed. of: Suicide, a cry for help.
    Includes bibliographical references.
    ISBN 0-8007-5929-X (pbk.)
    1. Suicide—United States—Psychological aspects. 2. Suicide—Religious aspects—Christianity. I. Hosier, Helen Kooiman. Suicide, a cry for help. II. Title.
HV6548.U5H63 2005
248.8′628—dc22   2005004676

Contents

Acknowledgments

Save me, and I will thank you publicly before the entire congregation, before the largest crowd I can find.

Psalm 35:18

This verse became my promise to God made after my failed suicide. At the time, my writing was rededicated to the Lord and the reading audience has become "the congregation . . . the largest crowd."

Thank you, dear Father, for rescuing me.

I will rejoice in the Lord. He shall rescue me! From the bottom of my heart praise rises to him.

Psalm 35: 9–10

Introduction

Suicide. The whispered word. The taboo subject. At one time it was labeled "going sideways." By any name, it is not a dinner table subject. If you can imagine it, by this time tomorrow, twenty-four hours from now, at least eighty-seven people will have died from suicide. That amounts to one suicide every seventeen minutes. Their deaths will be recorded as completed suicides, but another estimated 2,175 adults will have attempted to take their own lives. It is estimated that for every suicide there are twenty-five attempts for each death by suicide. In 2002 (the latest year for which there are national statistics), there were 31,656 suicides in the U.S. (These are the latest available statistics from the American Association of Suicidology.)

The very word *suicide* conjures up something from which we instinctively want to withdraw. Suicide is an insult to remaining family members, friends, and co-workers—to humanity, the community, and society in general. Suicide rates in the United States can best be characterized as mostly stable over time with a slight tendency toward decrease. More adults die from suicide than from homicide in the United States. Notice that this is just adults; it doesn't include child or teenage suicides.

The likelihood is that, at some point in your life, you will be confronted with the suicide or attempted suicide of someone you know. Each suicide intimately affects at least six other people. That seems like a low number when you consider family members, extended family, and friends. Turning aside from the problem is not going to solve or diminish the likelihood of it happening. Far better to take a serious look at it, discover what you can about it, and face the magnitude of the problem. Everything I have read on the subject states, in one way or another, that most suicidal individuals who receive help receive it from some nonprofessional person who was sensitive to their plight, heard their distress, and knew how to make an appropriate response. I don't like having to admit this—and my suicide attempt happened many years ago—but what I learned then, and have learned since, has shown me the need to be transparently open and honest.

Suicide appears in all age groups, in both sexes, and on every economic level, and there are no geographic boundaries. When I make that comment, people often respond in disbelief. "All ages? Children don't think about committing suicide . . ." Think again. Studies and statistics show that children, preteens, and young people are at risk for suicide far more than anyone can possibly imagine. Suicide is the sixth leading cause of death for children ages five to fourteen; it is the third leading cause of death for young people ages fifteen to twenty-four, behind unintentional injury and homicide. Many variables contribute to a child's wish to die. When children, adolescents, and young people commit suicide, they die before they have had an opportunity to experience a better life. These are sad, disillusioned, disheartened, desperately unhappy, wanting-to-die young persons. Why? That haunting one-word question hangs in the air, begging for an answer. (See chapter 9.)

Suicide among older people (age sixty-five and up, representing about 12.3 percent of the population) is of growing concern. Ill health, financial worries, the loss of one's spouse, and the resultant loneliness—these are distressingly real problems. The average suicide rate for this age category is one person every ninety-five minutes, accounting for about fifteen deaths each day. White males over the age of eighty-five take their own lives at a rate almost 5.5 times greater than for female suicide.

All of this, and more, is carefully dealt with in this book as I have examined this difficult subject out of a sense of urgent need, addressing what I see as a growing societal problem.

I have also addressed the subject of depression, a common but greatly misunderstood emotional illness that is often unrecognized and, therefore, undiagnosed. Some mental health professionals predict that by the year 2020 depression will be second only to heart disease as the world's most disabling illness. It is important to understand this, since most suicides are the result of depression. You cannot talk about suicide without addressing the subject of depression. According to the surgeon general, "Suicide is a complex behavior usually caused by a combination of factors. Research shows that almost all people who kill themselves have a diagnosable mental or substance abuse disorder or both, and that the majority have depressive illness. Studies indicate that the most promising way to prevent suicide and suicidal behavior is through the early recognition and treatment of depression and other psychiatric illnesses."[1]

My reasons for writing this book are, basically, three:

1. To offer understanding, empathy, and hope to those so overwhelmed by the vicissitudes of life that they have sought escape through suicide but have failed in their attempt.

2. To examine motives and lay bare some often overlooked facts regarding the "why" of suicide, depression, and mental illness. I'll also show some of the myths regarding suicide. My hope is that readers can gain an understanding of what drives a person to suicidal despair. To be aware of the problems accompanying depression and its potentially devastating consequences may be to become an intervenor and to help save a life. I have consistently found in the available literature on the subject of suicide that practicing clinical psychologists and those involved in suicide prevention strongly believe that increased awareness and a better understanding of the issues by society as a whole results in more effective suicide prevention.

3. To provide biblical counsel that can help move a person out of suicidal preoccupation and show that there is hope and a reason for living. I will show examples of biblical people who had the desire to die but who, with God's help, became overcomers. This book will not provide just religious answers telling you how to feel but will show you the compassion of Jesus, who, if he were here in bodily form, would wrap his arms around you and give comfort and courage.

Dr. Paul Pretzel's book *Understanding and Counseling the Suicidal Person* helped me gain an understanding of the role of religious beliefs in dealing with the subject of suicide. Dr. Pretzel says that, more and more, professionals dealing with the suicidal patient are becoming aware of the necessity of leading the patient to an affirmative belief in something of value. That being true, it is discomforting to find that the theological or religious meaning of suicide has been almost totally ignored in the past. That is something this book seeks to remedy, not from some lofty pinnacle of theological knowledge, but from firsthand experience with the subject and the knowledge that it is the Word of God that has seen me through crisis times. I give this to you out of genuine concern and in a spirit of love. I wish I could wrap my arms around you.

❧1❧

An Eclipse in My Soul

Suicide is not the stuff of melodrama, but a cry for help voiced in the cryptic language of loneliness and rejection.[1]

Norman Farberow, Ph.D.

I was tired beyond the telling, both physically and mentally. Every fiber of my being ached, nerves were taut, pressure had mounted to the exploding point, and the suffocatingly real depression I was feeling had settled in like a heavy, blanketing fog. My vision was obscured by the black pessimism of despair, and the future stretched before me as one long bout with loneliness. All I could see was work, loneliness, more work, and more lonely, difficult hours of struggle. Work, loneliness, tiredness—the thoughts cycled through my mind in ceaseless repetition. I had moved to a new community, hadn't made new friends, hadn't connected with a church or any community organization, and just the day before had put my eleven-year-old son on a plane to spend his summer vacation in Canada with his sister. I was very much alone, and now it was Friday night—the weekend lay ahead. But what was there for me, a lonely, recently divorced midforties woman?

In the back of my mind hovered the knowledge that God understood. He cared. But I was so weary of it all, the sameness of life every day. What did I have to look forward to? I had no doubt about the reality of God, but at this point I needed someone with skin on his face. All I wanted was a shoulder to lean on, someone else to help carry the load besides God. I felt starved for love. To write this now is to feel shame; nevertheless, it's how I felt, and I have since discovered that my experience is not uncommon. But the shame we feel is unwarranted. I didn't know it at the time.

I drove thirty-five miles from my home under a mammoth weight of despair. On arriving at my destination—the home of dear, loving friends who had remained steadfast and loyal—running to the front door, and ringing the bell, I discovered my friends were gone. I had thought for sure they would be there. I had hoped to collapse in their arms. I was so tired. I felt more alone than ever, rejected and unwanted. I was totally incapable of rational thought. I reached into the glove compartment of the car. There was the bottle of prescription sleeping pills I'd had filled that noon. Beside me was a can of cola. My last thought was a prayer: *God, please forgive me, but I'd rather be with you.*

Twelve hours later I awoke in my own bed. Was it a bad dream? A nightmare? No, I was fully clothed, and on my nightstand was the bottle of sleeping pills, an empty bottle!

I was now a statistic—a living statistic, to be sure. And I was not sure I was happy about it. "You are a walking miracle," the doctor declared. "The pills should have done it; and if they hadn't, the thirty-five-mile freeway drive back to your home certainly should have taken care of your desire to end it all. I don't understand how you drove your car back. If I never believed in angels before, I certainly do now. Your guardian angel worked overtime! I have a feeling someone up there wants you around alive awhile longer."

What had happened? How do you explain miracles? I don't know what happened or how I got home. Did I stop en route and regurgitate? I don't remember. Surely my guardian angel drove the car, but I simply do not know. But this I do know: God spared my life. God saved me. There had been an eclipse in my soul, but God brought me through. I was alive and comparatively well on planet Earth. There were no aftereffects whatsoever.

Now what was I going to do? Had I really wanted a permanent out? My mind struggled with questions. But there was work to do. Work! I hated the word. But it stared me in the face. Stacks of it. I was writing a major biography of a very well-known man. There was a fast-approaching deadline. I held down a full-time job, a new and very responsible position. I had a home to manage, children to consider. As I began to analyze my situation, I regained perspective. *Work is good therapy*, I told myself, and so I pitched in.

I received help from loving, concerned friends in whom I confided. They came immediately and took me to a doctor who lived in my community. The doctor called in a Christian psychologist. With his help I tried to look at my situation more objectively. Long, dark shadows had fallen across my path. Midnight hours.

Charles Swindoll, in *The Mystery of God's Will*, discloses that if he gets low or a little depressed, it happens when the sun goes down. If he has a battle, it usually occurs somewhere between sundown and bedtime. It rarely happens in the morning; there's something about the fresh dawn of a new day that brings back the hope he'd lost the night before. That's why it's called the "dark night of the soul." I identify with that. I had been in that kind of a valley, where the shadow was dark and frightening indeed.

Swindoll explains that in all his forty-plus years of ministering to troubled souls, he's observed that very few people take their lives in the early hours of dawn, that most suicides he's had to deal with take place when the sun goes down—at night, in the darkness, when life just caves in and hope disappears.

"Why is it when we lose all hope the enemy says, 'Take your life'? Why is it that the enemy's favorite option for desperate, hopeless people is suicide? Why, in the dark night of the soul, does he prompt, 'Put an end to it'?"[2]

Swindoll answers his question by pointing to Lamentations 3:22–23, where we are reminded that the Lord's mercies never cease; his compassions never fail. They are new every morning, and the Lord's faithfulness never diminishes. Swindoll asks, "Do you know what God's fresh, new morning message is to us?" I can answer that by telling you I experienced it. When the eclipse in my soul had passed, I recognized that the sun still rose each morning; the birds still chirped, awakening me; and the day's work was there to greet me. I walked through my darling house and out into the beautiful backyard ringed with huge, towering trees. My German shepherd romped around me, begging me to throw the frisbee, and I heard myself say, "Count your blessings. You have a loving heavenly Father who spared your life, who cares for you, and who has provided work for you to meet your needs and those of your children." Yes, God's mercy, his compassion, and his faithfulness were there for me, and they are there for you too.

Then alone I retreated into the psalms in the Bible. The psalmist became my companion. "Strange," you say. "You shake your fist in the face of God and try to kill yourself, and then you read the Bible?" Strange perhaps, but true. I discovered that David, who wrote many of the psalms, had his highs and lows. In the crucible of daily living, David soared to heights of joy and plummeted to the depths of despair.

In his pilgrimage from doubt to certainty, in his conquest of despair, he laid bare his heart. In the psalms I sought refuge and found the help I needed to sustain me through the difficult hours. The gamut of human experience is reflected in those psalms—anguish and guilt, gloom and apprehension, fear, pain, grief, sadness, and weariness. All this and much more spoke to my aching heart. And, oh, how I identified!

In my copy of *The Living Bible*, the book of Psalms is underlined and circled. There are exclamation points and little notes, all a solemn reminder, even today, that God saw me and took me through this crisis in my soul. Some of those underlined excerpts read like this:

> Death bound me with chains, and the floods of ungodliness mounted a massive attack against me. Trapped and helpless, I struggled against the ropes that drew me on to death. In my distress I screamed to the Lord for his help. And he heard me from heaven; my cry reached his ears. . . . He sped swiftly to my aid. . . . Suddenly the brilliance of his presence broke through the clouds. . . . He reached down from heaven and took me and drew me out of my great trials. He rescued me from deep waters. He delivered me. . . . The Lord held me steady. He led me to a place of safety, for he delights in me.
>
> Psalm 18:4–6, 10, 12, 16–19

I remember stopping when I read, "He delights in me." Was it really true? *Me?* I knew the Bible was a timeless book; its very timelessness made it applicable to every age of history. So it did include *me*. I read on:

> You have turned on my light! The Lord my God has made my darkness turn to light. Now in your strength I can scale any wall, attack any troop. What a God he is! How perfect in every way! All his promises prove true. He is a shield for

everyone who hides behind him. For who is God except our
Lord? Who but he is as a rock?

Psalm 18:28–31

Oh, how I needed a strong rock to lean against. There followed long periods of anguish when I poured out my heart
to the God the psalmist said cares for me in my distress—to
the God who is merciful.

Lord! Help!

Psalm 12:1

Lord, lead me as you promised me you would. . . . Tell me
clearly what to do, which way to turn.

Psalm 5:8

The psalmist's cries became my cries. God was at work
directing my turning. One does not jump up from trying to
go sideways and immediately walk a straight, steady line. I
limped, struggled, stumbled. Sometimes I fell down. Then
again I would cry out like David:

Pity me, O Lord, for I am weak. Heal me, for my body is
sick, and I am upset and disturbed. My mind is filled with
apprehension and with gloom. Oh, restore me soon. . . .
Every night my pillow is wet with tears. . . . I am depend-
ing on you, O Lord my God.

Psalms 6:2–3, 6; 7:1

It was not a misplaced dependence. God could be depended
upon to heal the hurting me.

Mark this well: The Lord . . . will listen to me and answer
when I call to him. Stand before the Lord in awe, and do not
sin against him. Lie quietly upon your bed in silent medi-
tation. Put your trust in the Lord, and offer him pleasing

sacrifices. Many say that God will never help us. Prove them wrong, O Lord, by letting the light of your face shine down upon us. . . . I will lie down in peace and sleep, for though I am alone, O Lord, you will keep me safe.

Psalm 4:3–6, 8

From one who has been there, you can take it as truth: he is a God who helps, he is a God who can be trusted, and he is a God who keeps us safe. When we are alone, as so many are, he is a reality.

I made many discoveries in those days coming up out of the pit of despair. The psalmist's mood in the Bible so often fit mine. He reflected my own spirit. There was release from my own deep inner hurt as I, with the writer, lay my wounded spirit at the feet of God. A woman I recently met related that when she learned her son had opted for the homosexual lifestyle and contracted AIDS and then her daughter revealed she had a lesbian partner, she found herself so distraught that she sought refuge in the book of Psalms. "Those psalms saved me," she confessed, "saved me from deep depression that might have resulted in suicide."

I, likewise, had been saved from myself. I began slowly to see that I was my own worst enemy, that in giving way to self-pity and surrendering to black moods of depression, I was shutting myself up to the love and help I so desperately craved. I needed to take myself in hand and then hand myself over to God. In those days I found myself saying, "Dear God, you are really getting the short end of this deal. I'm such a miserable bargain." Believe me, I found out that God doesn't mind!

David, in the psalms, told me that God is my shield and that he will defend me. I discovered that God is a judge who is perfectly fair. Over and over again the psalmist told me that God is good, *so good*. David said to this God of good-ness, "I cannot understand how you can bother with mere puny man, to pay any attention to him!" (Ps. 8:4). That same

21

thought frequently crossed my mind. Out of the fullness of his heart, David exclaimed, "O Lord, I will praise you with all my heart, and tell everyone about the marvelous things you do. I will be glad, yes, filled with joy because of you. . . . You have vindicated me; you have endorsed my work, declaring from your throne that it is good" (Ps. 9:1–2, 4).

And to think that I thought I needed someone else to help carry the load besides God! Shame engulfed me, remorse for my foolish act. David reminded me that all who are oppressed may come to the Lord, that he is a refuge for them in their times of trouble. David showed me God's mercy, that he can be counted on for help and that he has never forsaken those who trust in him (Ps. 9:9–10).

David told me, "Tell the world about his unforgettable deeds" (Ps. 9:11). I was a writer. Was God trying to get a message across to me? I had been told that if I divorced, God couldn't use me anymore, that my days as a Christian writer were ended, that no one would ever publish me again. Now I heard myself crying, "You mean, God, you aren't through with me? You mean I can still write, and someone will still publish me?"

I found Psalm 35:18 and was literally stopped in my tracks. There I read, "Save me, and I will thank you publicly before the entire congregation, before the largest crowd I can find." I knew my life had been spared. God had saved me. I cried out to God, "Father, I *will* do that. I *can* do that. With your help I *will* use this gift of writing that you have entrusted to me to point others to you. Father, the largest crowd I can find that I can conceive of would be through writing." The gift was dedicated to the Lord, and with his help, I have sought always to use it for him. At that juncture in my life, six books had been written and published; today, as I write this, there are more than sixty published books. God! Only God! He forgives, he forgets, he redeems, he is merciful! He restores.

When David said that he felt hopeless, overwhelmed, and in deep distress and that his problems seemed to go from bad to worse (Ps. 25:16), I, as a woman alone, making the adjustment to a new job in a strange community, could feel some of the guilt about my suicide attempt slip away. Here was a man after God's own heart making that kind of confession:

See my sorrows; feel my pain; forgive my sin. . . . Save me from them! Deliver [me] from their power! Oh, let it never be said that I trusted you in vain! . . . Assign me Godliness and Integrity as my bodyguards, for I expect you to protect me and to ransom [me] from all [my] troubles.

Psalm 25:18, 20–22

In my mind's eye, I pictured David lifting his hands to heaven, imploring God's help. And just as God didn't ignore his cry, I knew he would help me too. David, to our knowledge, did not make an attempt on his own life, but he must have felt like it many times. When you are the object of a schizophrenic king's hatred, when you are rejected by your countrymen and your favorite son (who tried to usurp your kingdom), when you lose your best friend, when you are faced with marital problems (and David had many wives), when you are confronted with your own sins and the magnitude of your own willfulness, when you are charged with the responsibility of having to make grave decisions of far-reaching importance, and when you have to face the death of loved ones, you will experience moments of deep anguish. Out of all this, David wrote the psalms.

As I read God's response to David, the words of the doctor kept ringing in my head: *"You are a walking miracle. . . . I have a feeling someone up there wants you around alive awhile longer."* Many times since then, even when things have been very difficult, I have been able to say, "It's good to be alive!"

❊ 2 ❊

Could Something Be Missing?

Hope moves a person out of suicidal preoccupation.[1]

Earl Grollman

You can read it in books, articles, and research papers: in the absence of hope, faith flounders. J. Wallace Hamilton, in his book *What About Tomorrow?* first snagged my attention with this statement. Hamilton was referring more specifically to a religious faith, but in broader terms it could include faith in one's friends, one's relatives, one's husband or wife, and even one's job, or faith that tomorrow will be better. Stress in interpersonal relationships, leading to loneliness, alienation, or isolation from others, is one of the leading factors contributing to suicide. Hope disappears from the horizon. And the most important hope of all—hope in God and his plan for one's life—may never have existed at all or, if it did, was momentarily obscured by the gravity of the suicidal person's situation.

J. B. Phillips, one of my all-time favorite writers and transla-
tors, helped me see that religion merely as religion is useless,
that the worship of God is empty unless it is coupled with
justice and compassion toward others and the right kind of
love toward God and self. Jesus emphasized this again and
again by his life, his example, and we have the Bible, which
holds out the highest hope if we will but turn to it and ab-
sorb its message into our deepest, innermost being. Staying
God-focused will keep us on track. The value of a sustaining
religious faith cannot be emphasized sufficiently.

One of the things a strong faith does is help us to trust—and
basic human trust is a distinct human need. Lacking such
faith, people must seek basic trust from other sources. Suicidal
persons have failed in this. Disillusionment and a form of
emotional starvation overtakes them. For many it is of limited
duration, but it overpowers rational decision making, and they
succumb to their pain and act on their impulse to end it all.

Only a small proportion of suicidal people call an agency
or a professional for help. As stated in my introduction, most
are lost somewhere in the general population not knowing
where to turn or how to deal with their intensive, overwhelming feelings. If they are to be helped, it will be because some
nonprofessional person was sensitive to their plight, heard
their distress, and knew how to make an appropriate response.[2]
I repeat here for emphasis. And that, of course, is what this
book seeks to do, to help you know how to make an appropriate response.

Suicide: Always a Cry for Help

I recall with gratitude the telephone call I received shortly
after the first edition of this book was published. It was from
a layman friend, an editor at a publishing house, whose voice

clearly conveyed his emotions: "Helen, if I hadn't read your book, I'm not so sure I would have understood what was going on in my friend's life. . . . I had just finished reading your book, thank God, and recognized John's call as a definite cry for help. I was able to get to him in time, and his life was saved." In the years that followed, over and over again I received letters and phone calls, or people would say something similar to me in person.

After my own failed suicide, I began to look into what others have written and said about the subject. It was at this juncture in my life that I met Duane Pederson, who had an incredible ministry outreach to street people in Hollywood, California. Duane's work continues to this day, a wonderful helping ministry.[3] He published a newspaper called the *Hollywood Free Paper*, which was distributed at no charge and reached across the country. In it he shared stories of the "Jesus People," the term he coined for young people who were having life-changing experiences as they encountered the reality of Jesus. Duane began receiving letters, hundreds of them. It seemed that the majority related the same heartbreaking story of attempted suicide. Some wrote about friends' completed suicides. This was heavy, heavy stuff and all too real.

As we read these letters, Duane and I began to see the need to address the subject, and we did so in a book entitled *Going Sideways*. This present book is an outgrowth of that original research and my ongoing awareness that suicide is a much-neglected subject and that, once again, the time to speak up about it is *now*. Those letters began to take on a familiar ring. One of them read, "Within the last year three of my friends tried to commit suicide. Life was too much for them. They couldn't hack it. This world ate them up until their only thought of escape was death. Could something be missing?"

That question was echoed in one way or another in these hundreds of letters; it is a question that I have seen in media accounts of suicide through the years.

Is Suicide the Ultimate Geographic Cure?

To ask if suicide is the ultimate geographic cure raises many questions. If someone is longing for an ultimate better location, he is well advised to consider the warning one minister gave to a would-be suicide who was denying the reality of God and an eternity that would be spent in one of two places. This pastor told the man that if he persisted in trying to take his own life, the place he would go was far worse than the situation he presently found himself in here on earth. "You had better stay around and find God's solution for your dilemma!" he kindly admonished.

You may be thinking that was too harsh a statement, that it doesn't seem kind. Suicidal behavior should be understood as a manifestation of the person's need for some basic change in his or her life. The pastor was using a shock approach to divert the man's thinking, and it worked. The threat of suicide, or the act itself, is always a cry for help. It has been described as a cry directed to the significant others in the suicidal person's life sphere, but it can also be seen as a cry of spiritual desperation—a cry to God.

In this instance, the pastor was able to tell the man about the experiences of Dr. Maurice Rawlings, a specialist in internal medicine and cardiovascular diseases at the Diagnostic Hospital in Chattanooga, Tennessee, who began documenting a series of interviews with people who had been resuscitated—brought back to life after being clinically dead. What Dr. Rawlings found supports belief in life after death and the existence of a hell as well as a heaven. In his book, *Be-*

yond Death's Door, Dr. Rawlings stated, "More and more of my patients who are recovering from serious illnesses tell me there is life after death. There is a heaven and a hell. I had always thought of death as painless extinction. I had bet my life on it. Now I have had to reconsider my own destiny, and what I have found isn't good. I have found it really may not be safe to die!"[4]

The turnaround in this doctor's life occurred when a patient had a cardiac arrest and dropped dead right in the doctor's office. In the process of resuscitation, as he regained his heartbeat and respiration, the man started screaming, "I'm in hell." He was terrified and pleaded with the doctor to help him.

Dr. Rawlings worked feverishly and rapidly, and the man's life was saved. In the process, however, both the patient and the doctor came to grips with the reality of hell. "I had always dealt with death as a routine occurrence in my medical practice, regarding it as an extinction with no need for remorse or apprehension. Now I was convinced there was something about this life and death business after all. All of my concepts needed revision. I needed to find out more. It was like finding another piece in the puzzle that supports the truth of the Scriptures. I was discovering that the Bible was not merely a history book. Every word was turning out to be true."[5] I met Dr. Rawlings at the time he was writing this book, so I can attest to the validity of what he experienced and wrote about.

A number of books have been published relating the death experiences of scores of people. But most of these books would have the reader believe that at the end of the tunnel marked "death" there is this bright light and pleasurable experiences. All will be well in that life beyond. But that is not the case if one isn't prepared to meet God.

On the Edge of Eternity

The pastor served as an intervenor, and his intervention helped the man rethink life and the hereafter. I have never been able to dismiss lightly the need to give serious thought to the hereafter. Years ago I was introduced to the writings of A. W. Tozer and was captivated. In his best-selling book *The Knowledge of the Holy*, he wrote, "We who live in this nervous age would be wise to meditate on our lives and our days long and often before the face of God and on the edge of eternity. For we are made for eternity as certainly as we are made for time, and as responsible moral beings we must deal with both."[6]

Some years ago I met Roald and Wilma Stanchfield, a Minnesota couple who had been struck by lightning and survived the horror of that experience, even though a direct hit is almost always fatal. That this couple survived was miraculous. Both of them relate the death-tunnel experience, the bright light, and an encounter with the glory of God. But they also tell of falling away from the brilliant light and knowing they were not going to heaven. Wilma asks, "Do you have any idea what it feels like to die when you do not know God?" They were on their way to a Christless eternity.

As they lay in hospital beds, Roald said to his wife, "Wilma, there really is a God." They recognized that something was missing in their lives. I had the privilege of writing their story: *Struck by Lightning, Then by Love*. In it Wilma said, "I was headed into eternity with everything that had ever been wrong in my life—it was a heavy load—and I was being separated from God. It was not at all glorious, and I did not feel the comforting presence of anyone. I was never so alone in my entire life as I was in that moment."[7] Since that experience, Wilma has had a tremendous ministry of outreach speaking for Christian women's clubs and at retreats and events nation-wide. Her message is one of hope as she seeks to introduce hearers to Jesus, who was the missing dimension in her and her husband's lives.

A. W. Tozer speaks of this so eloquently: "God's eternity and man's mortality join to persuade us that faith in Jesus Christ is not optional. For every man it must be Christ or eternal tragedy. Out of eternity our Lord came into time to rescue His human brethren whose moral folly had made them not only fools of the passing world but slaves of sin and death as well."[8]

The Three H's and Suicide as an Emergency Exit

The generalized cause of suicide has been attributed to the three H's—haplessness, helplessness, and hopelessness. The hapless person feels the cards are stacked against him or her along with tough-luck events. The person is lonely and feels helpless to do anything about his or her situation. About that time he or she loses all hope. The three H's converge, and the person is then likely to consider suicide as an emergency exit that frees him or her from the immediate present and the inevitable tomorrow with its pain and problems.

Reasons and the Dark Abyss of Pessimism

Gathering up the statistics and available data, one is struck by one thing—the common thread of hopelessness surrounding the victim's life. At one time it was erroneously thought that everyone who committed suicide was mentally deranged, but that has been disproved. It is known, however, that the person attempting suicide is always desperate, one who has lost all hope. A typical suicide letter will state, "At this point I've reached an all-time low in my life. My creative drives and ambitions have seemingly evaporated. I've never felt so alone. I feel as though I haven't one friend in the world. I know I'm giving in to self-pitying despair. But I feel so helpless in this hopeless situation. What can I do? I'm at the end of my rope."

Here are some factors contributing to suicide: feelings of incompetence and failure, lack of resources, no apparent open paths, guilty feelings, repressed rage, sadness, interpersonal difficulties, marital problems, serious illness, job reversals, excessive use of barbiturates, postalcoholic withdrawal, advancing age, and the problems of the elderly. All of these things find individuals groping their way through what becomes a dark abyss of pessimism that ends in deep depression and suicide. Tired of stumbling over the debris of broken dreams and unfulfilled plans, these people feel that life has become a long, grim race, and they don't feel up to staying in the running.

He Is Not a Little God

J. B. Phillips, in *Your God Is Too Small*, talks about our misconceptions and how we may find ourselves thinking that the God who is responsible for the terrifying vastness of the universe cannot possibly be interested in the lives of the minute specks of consciousness that exist on this insignificant planet.

Ever feel that way? Phillips says we feel cast adrift in this vast sea of humanity, and who is there to care? Our whole sphere of life is so minute by comparison that we cannot conceive of God taking interest in that which is of such concern to us. But, ah, that's just it—we have a concept of an inadequate God. He is not a little God! He is a very big God, but he is a loving, understanding heavenly Father as well. Don't try to comprehend it. Accept it. He is much more than an infinitely magnified human being.

Phillips's book was in my possession at the time I went through the slough of despondency. I read it—no, I devoured it. I came to see that God is an adequate God. More than adequate, he is enough, and Jesus was the embodiment of God in human history. It's easy to stumble in the dark, but when light comes on the scene, there is no need to grope. The light of God's love penetrated the darkness of my thinking. As I refocused my thoughts on what I knew to be true—that God *is* and that I could trust him to see me through—and got my eyes off myself and the immediate situation confronting me, I was able to go on. He will do that for you too.

❧ 3 ❧

Nancy and Failed
Suicide Attempts

Life is a battle in which we fall from the wounds we receive
in running away.

John Rannell

I need to tell you Nancy's story. Please be aware that this
chapter tells a disturbing story. It reveals many things that
need to be confronted in difficult situations, and failure
to confront these things can lead to the kind of tragedy and
heartache described here. This story raises questions about
generational bondage and failure to admit to depression and
the need for professional help. When families sweep problems
under the proverbial rug, the rug becomes very lumpy. Was
the family pastor called for counsel? Would he have been able
to provide what was needed? Would he have recognized the

need for family members to receive Christian psychological counseling? Would family members even have admitted that they needed help? But first the story.

Nancy lived alone in a large southern city. She was blind and a failed suicide. She failed not once, nor twice, but three times in trying to kill herself. Her story is doubly tragic in that on her third suicide try, Nancy succeeded only in blinding herself. John Rannell's statement, quoted at the outset of this chapter, showed itself to be only too real in Nancy's life. She was attempting to run away from life each time she tried to kill herself. God spared her life, and finally she began to see in a way she never saw before she became blind. Here's a warning: Don't try running away. Hold on. Give God time; give yourself time. Nancy learned this. You don't want to be another Nancy, blinded by a foolish act.

In the first edition of this book, I called Nancy by the name of Linda. She was still living at the time, but death finally claimed Nancy many years later when she died of cancer. I want to call her by her rightful name now, because I know she would want me to reveal her story in all its pathos. Both Nancy and her parents are with the Lord. Nancy's parents were dear friends of ours, Christian booksellers with a wide-ranging ministry of helps. Because I was a writer and often in need of someone to transcribe interview cassette tapes, Nancy's mother suggested I use her daughter's services. "She's an excellent typist; we'll check to make sure she's doing it right, but it would give her something to do and provide inspiration and a reason for still living." And so Nancy became my right-hand help, even when we moved out of the city where she lived, and for ten or more years, she transcribed literally hundreds of interview tapes for me. It is safe to say that I used Nancy's services for at least nineteen of my books. Nancy's life was salvaged; we became the closest of friends.

But the real tragedy is that this woman was so bound by her fears, so enslaved to her emotions, and so intent on slashing her way through the jungle that was her life that she failed to see what was missing in her life before she tried to take it. Unable to see or create alternatives to what was happening, she felt trapped in hopelessness and helplessness. Did she admit to anyone that she needed help? No. Did she even admit to herself that she needed help? No. God was adequate to help her, but she failed to reach out. Instead, she thought only of escape.

Blinded So She Could See

Nancy's marriage was a mistake from the beginning. She suffered at the hands of an abusive husband who mistreated not only her but their children.

Nancy was not unlike many women who contemplate or complete suicide. Because of her two previous suicide attempts, certain family members and some so-called friends had Nancy believing she was so emotionally disturbed that she was beyond help and hope. A huge mistake! When a person is down and out, you don't heap condemnation or critical analysis on him or her. Six weeks after a hysterectomy, Nancy experienced some physical problems that caused her great anxiety. She never revealed to me why she had that anxiety. She related, "I sat in the doctor's office awaiting my turn. I remember thinking this time that my physical problems might lead to a lingering death that would require caregivers and only bring more heartache to my already troubled children and my parents. My children had suffered enough. We were all subjected to physical abuse, beatings, and verbal lashings. My husband had a terrible temper. I withheld all this from my parents, however, and lived a lie. Divorce was unthinkable in our family with its strong Christian roots. I couldn't bring that kind of disgrace upon my parents. Yet the day came when I simply had to get out of that abusive relationship, and subsequent to my suicide attempts, the divorce did become final. I felt like the black sheep of the family."

There was a time when the stigma of divorce was so awful in the Christian world that for the most part it simply wasn't done. I myself experienced the fallout from that kind of stigmatizing. Nancy was only too aware of what a divorce could do to her standing in the Christian community, and also how it would affect her parents. Better to live a lie, she thought, so she never even revealed to her parents what she and her children were suffering at the hands of her abusive husband. She did finally get a divorce; it was after that when she made two failed attempts to take her life. What happened to Nancy? It was a crisis of faith. She was seeing "through a glass darkly." God hadn't abandoned her. She was in a crisis involving many changes; she needed help. She failed to seek it. Those closest to her were not keeping close enough tabs on her to know what was going on. Another mistake. We need significant others in our lives.

Nancy said, "That day while waiting in the doctor's office, as I thought about the possibility of a slow death—because I felt the prognosis on my condition wasn't going to be good and that it was just a matter of time—I got up and left the office. To myself I thought, *The children and my parents can adjust to a quick death much easier.* I knew what I could do. This time I'd make certain I didn't fail. I didn't say anything to anyone; I just left the doctor's office without a word."

Nancy's experience with God was, she felt, real. By the standards of others, she would have been considered very zealous in her religious beliefs. Dr. Archibald Hart, in *Un-*

masking Male Depression, explains that depression, not God, makes you feel distant from God, as if he has interposed a thick ceiling between you and him. The first thing anyone who is depressed has to get straight is that you cannot trust your feelings. God is not abandoning you; you are abandoning God because of your depressed feelings.

Nancy's story continues: "I went home, and I remember thinking, *God said we had to bear nothing we could not bear.* I could not bear to see my kids suffer anymore, and since I'd never had an illness unto death, I'd take care of that. The house was in order, and I dressed in a dress that I liked very much, so I felt ready to go. I got the gun out and then decided to take two sleeping pills so it wouldn't hurt so much in case it wasn't instant. I went to the bedroom and lay down. I picked up the gun and held it to my temple."

After she pulled the trigger, she didn't die; she didn't even lose consciousness. She told me, "I thought, *God, you will not even let me die. Now what?*" Her anger was misdirected. In her rational mind she would never have lashed out at God. "The telephone kept ringing and ringing. I thought it would never quit. I didn't answer it. God and I were having a silent argument, and I remember thinking, *Well, at least you are talking to me even if it is to say you are going to have your way.* The telephone kept ringing. Would it ever stop? At last it did. There was still a very silent struggle going on within me. I would not give up without a battle. But neither would I call for help. I had pulled the trigger at 2:00 p.m. When I finally did call a friend, I learned it was early the next morning. The telephone was in the living room, and I do not remember seeing, but neither do I remember thinking that I could not see. I groped my way to the phone and then to the door and unlocked it so my friend could get in. Then I returned to the bedroom."

Why hadn't Nancy thought about how this would affect her children (grown, married, and with families of their own) and her parents? Once again we see the irrational thinking that can take over when someone is depressed and becomes suicidal.

There followed a long stay in the hospital during which Nancy underwent surgery and neurological and psychological testing. She recounted, "I saw two psychiatrists. Understandably, my anxiety through all of this was great. There was also functional testing that indicated loss of some control in the use of my fingers." The testing itself, however, revealed that Nancy was not considered psychopathic. The testing revealed many things about her that bolstered her self-esteem and her confidence that she could rebuild her life and help her children regain stability. But Nancy's sight was permanently gone. She received the help that enabled her to understand her situation after the fact, after the third failed suicide. Back then, more than thirty years ago, people were not as inclined to seek psychological counseling or even to confide in their pastors. In reading Dr. Hart's book, I heard myself say, "Yes! Yes!" as I read,

> There is so much misunderstanding, and even fear, surrounding the treatment of depression that my goal . . . is to demystify the treatment process and show that it is not only very straightforward and scientific but does not run contrary to any of our cherished biblical principles. The resistance to the treatment of depression that exists in the minds of even the most intelligent of Christians is not justified. . . . The fear of treatment . . . has kept many pulpits busy trying to prevent those with deep depression from reaching effective help. It is profoundly sad to me that such emotional abuse through ignorance is perpetuated in the name of Christ.
>
> Yet there is a glimmer of hope. One of the things I do these days is teach seminars for pastors. And everywhere I go, *almost*

everyone who hears what I have to say becomes convinced that we are allowing Satan to use our resistance and ignorance to gain the upper hand.[1]

Nancy's story continues: "It is hard to express the feelings of relief. Now I knew without a doubt that I was of a sound mind. With the Lord's help I had been able to withstand the onslaughts of 'friends' and family members who did not comprehend and who judged the divorce and me in such a terrible way. God saw me through this crisis experience. I knew from that time on that my strength lay in the Lord. I was released as mentally healthy and completely competent. The Lord blessed me with good doctors—men of integrity and thoughtfulness. It had always been easier for me to face concrete obstacles rather than unknown ones, but now I could also face the unknown without despair or resentment. I asked for God's forgiveness and had the assurance in my heart that he understood and forgave me. My healing was complete even though I would remain blind." The counsel Nancy received from competent professionals put her back on her feet physically and emotionally.

Asking for God's forgiveness was part of the healing of her depression, and God restored her to usefulness so that she could think well of herself, contribute to her living expenses, and not feel she was a burden to her parents and married children.

This question needs to be addressed: why was Nancy a target for an abusive husband in the first place? Nancy did not understand the biblical model for the role of husbands and wives (see 1 Pet. 3:1–7). Erroneous teaching about submission had placed her in an untenable position. Husbands are to love their wives as Christ loved the church, not lord it over them with physical and verbal abuse. And not only Nancy but her children were subjected to such abuse. Moreover, Nancy feared what her parents, other family members, and friends would say if she told them what was going on. Another huge mistake. Anyone who is the target of such abuse needs to report it and get help.

The Effect on Nancy's Parents

The act of suicide often stigmatizes the victim's survivors and raises many questions: "Why? Where have I failed? How can I now face people? What will others think?" I talked with Nancy's parents about this. "What emotions did you experience?" I asked. "How did you respond to Nancy, her children, and others?"

Her mother said, "After Nancy's first and second suicide attempts, we thought she would never attempt anything like that again. At the time she felt it was the way to solve her problems and that the children would be better off. We didn't know about the extensive cruelty that had been in the home before the marriage ended in a divorce. Later Nancy opened up her heart and told us all that had been going on for years.

"One morning my husband and I were having our devotions, and the phone rang. I shall never forget the look on his face when he came back to me. 'Nancy has shot herself; they want us to come to the hospital as quickly as possible.' Somehow through our big-city, early-morning rush-hour traffic, we got there.

"Nancy had shot herself the previous afternoon and had spent the night in her home alone. When she finally knew she wasn't going to die, she called for help. When I learned these details, it seemed inconceivable to me that I had been sleeping peacefully in my home all night with my daughter lying in her bed in her apartment having put a gun to her temple, hoping to kill herself. The bullet passed through the area just above her nose—in the area of the brain where the senses for tasting and smelling are. She had surgery. I shall never forget the Sunday some weeks later when the doctor came in and said, 'We are going to take you to another room,' and he took off the bandages and turned on the most brilliant light I have ever seen. He said to our daughter, 'What do you see?' and she responded, 'Nothing at all.'

"Nancy determined that if she was going to be blind the rest of her life, she would be as independent as possible. She overcame terrific obstacles—she went to the school for the blind, lives alone, and is self-sufficient. She has grown in the Scriptures and spends hours listening to tapes of the Bible in various translations and paraphrases. As the years have gone by, she has become a blessing to many people through her letter writing, her telephone counseling, her transcribing of your interview tapes, and her outreach to others."

Depression, Discouragement, and Suicide

The devil, our sworn enemy, has been "a murderer from the beginning" (John 8:44). If this enemy can succeed in destroying one of God's children, he has scored a great victory. It was Jim Elliot, martyred missionary to Ecuador, who wrote in his diary, "Discouragement is a satanic tool that seems to fit my disposition very well and the enemy knows it."[2] Nancy came to understand the enemy's devious tactics and how much God loved her in sparing her life again. With that realization came a determination to allow him to use her to help others.

But Nancy's experience had an effect on her parents as well. Her mother told me, "It was one of the most difficult things for me to face that I have ever encountered. We worked with the public and were constantly rubbing shoulders with people.

On one occasion a young man said to me, 'I'm praying for your daughter,' and I said, 'Which one? We have three.' He responded, 'The one who shot herself.' It was very, very difficult for me to admit that people knew what had happened, and I said to my husband, 'We should sell our Christian bookstore and get out. After all, if we have a daughter who has done a thing like trying to kill herself, what will people think and say?'

"At that time our attention was directed to a radio pastor, Theodore Epp, who helped a father deal with those same kinds of feelings. This father had gone to this pastor saying, 'I can't go on. Our son has done these terrible things,' and Theodore Epp said, 'That's just what the devil wants—don't go on; don't go on.'

"Hearing that gave me the backbone to know that the Lord was in this with all of us and that he had placed us in a position where, because of our daughter's experience, we could reach out to help hundreds. Our daughter was blinded so she could see, and not only her but us—after that we began to see things differently too." Nancy's parents, as well as Nancy, became voices of love to ease the pain of others.

What will people think? As Christians, we get stuck in that mode of thinking far too often. Nancy thought it for years, concealing as she did the marital discord and disharmony in the home. It was one of her parents' first reactions after the senseless tragedy that blinded their daughter. Good did come out of all this; God is in the restoration business. The story raises many questions about God and our relationship to him. As Nancy's heavenly parent, God must have grieved as he saw what was taking place. Be assured, God loves you and it is not in his best plan for your life that you go through what Nancy did. Jeremiah 29:11–13 is etched into my thinking: "'For I

42

know the plans I have for you,' declares the LORD, 'plans to prosper you and not to harm you, plans to give you hope and a future. Then you will call upon me and come and pray to me, and I will listen to you. You will seek me and find me when you seek me with all your heart'" (NIV).

Each of Us Is Important to God

We hear from the apostle Peter, who was hounded by Satan, "Be careful—watch out for attacks from Satan, your great enemy. He prowls around like a hungry, roaring lion, looking for some victim to tear apart. Stand firm when he attacks. Trust the Lord" (1 Pet. 5:8–9).

You are important to God. Each of us is. We are his children, his greatly loved created offspring. He has no favorites. Let this become imprinted upon your thinking. As 1 John 3:1 teaches, "See how very much our heavenly Father loves us, for he allows us to be called his children—think of it—and we really are!" This letter of the beloved apostle is called the family epistle, because it takes the child of God across the threshold into the fellowship of the Father's home.

Peter said that suffering and attacks from the enemy would come, but he promised that "God, who is full of kindness through Christ, will . . . come and pick you up, and set you firmly in place, and make you stronger than ever" (1 Pet. 5:10). When you think about the context in which Peter was writing such words—the persecution, the uncertainty, the martyrdoms among those early Christians—you have to acknowledge that God's power to work on behalf of his children has not diminished. "Trust yourself to the God who made you, for he will never fail you" (1 Pet. 4:19). Peter's words are meant for us today.

❧ 4 ❧

The Sorrow We Cannot Speak

When pressed with burdens and troubles too complicated to put into words and too mysterious to tell or understand, how sweet it is to fall back into His blessed arms, and just sob out the sorrow that we cannot speak.

L. B. Cowman, *Streams in the Desert*

T ragedy of tragedies—and strange as it may seem—neither Nancy nor her parents could help Nancy's beautiful daughter, a lovely blue-eyed blonde, married and the mother of two little boys. A crisis reveals what a person is made of, and this family went through several crisis experiences that would have sent people with small faith reeling and not recovering. Nancy's mother revealed what happened like this: "Our precious granddaughter, Gail, couldn't overcome the things of her childhood, they had been so terrible. One day she said to me, 'Grandmother, I'm going to kill myself.'

44

"I said, 'Oh no! You can't do that.' I pointed out to her how much she had to live for. But the day came when our daughter received a phone call from Gail."

The shrill ring of the phone was not unusual at Nancy's place, since she was doing so much telephone counseling for a nationwide television ministry. But the call on July 29, 1979, was forever stamped in Nancy's memory: "Gail, my darling daughter, so unique to this world, so lovely to look at, Gail who had built such defenses against an insecure world, terrified at times, radiantly happy at other times, was now calling to tell me good-bye. She said she was leaving this world, but I refused to believe it, even when she told me she'd taken all her heart medicine. She had just done it and received help very shortly, for I immediately called my father, who drove to her home a short distance away. Even while I talked to her, the pain in her chest increased. Her body, so beautiful but so fragile, could not make it.

"My father found her in the bathroom, where she had gone to throw up. I had told her to put her fingers down her throat and make herself gag. But she never regained consciousness."

I took time out from my work and flew to be with Nancy and her family at the time of Gail's death. What I saw was a courageous family bonded together by this senseless tragedy. At the time of Gail's suicide, Nancy had been transcribing tapes for me on one of the books I was writing. Just the day before, she'd called to say how blessed she'd been by hearing something on one of those tapes: "Courage comes without banners; courage comes without armies. Courage comes silent as an oak tree to those who ask it of God." As Nancy spoke to me over the phone, relating this heartbreak, I read those words as I had written them down, and I silently prayed that God would give this grieving family the courage they needed to go on.

Strong and beautiful as stately oak trees—that was the picture I carried with me of this courageous family who had experienced this terrible loss but who, even in their grief, were reaching out to console others. They could not know at that time how much they would need courage in the days ahead.

What a Difference Faith Makes!

Warren Wiersbe, in *Why Us? When Bad Things Happen to God's People*, explains that what life does to us depends a great deal on what life finds in us. The furnace of suffering and sadness has a way of testing the genuineness of our relationship with God. Oh, how my friends' faith was being tested! "What a difference faith makes!" Nancy said, recalling James 1, which speaks of our faith being tried and how this can result in patience. "I am very aware of God's presence and his ongoing love and help to me," Nancy said. "He will do for all of us what is needful and best."

Gail's death was a tragedy of monstrous proportions, and no one, including myself, tried to explain it or offer small-talk consolation. It was enough that we could put our arms around each other and sob out the sorrow we could not speak. I knew that even the angels in heaven must have been weeping as we stood together at Gail's grave.

In one of our telephone conversations, Nancy was able to talk of the terrible pain Gail had experienced with memories of the relationship with her father. Nancy and her parents didn't deny the pain or the loss they were feeling. And once again, now separated by miles so that I could not offer the comfort of my arms around Nancy's frail shoulders, I didn't try to rush in with feeble, fatuous words. We talked about the comfort to be found in the psalms and in other favorite passages. In particular, I remember the comfort we both experienced as we recalled Jesus's words, "Blessed are those who mourn, for they will be comforted" (Matt. 5:4 NIV).

"Go ahead and mourn, Nancy," my husband and I told her. "You will be blessed and comforted. Cry. God is keeping your tears in his bottle marked 'Nancy.'" (The reference was to Psalm 56:8.)

The Torment of Painful Memories

If ever there was a time for Nancy to remember Jesus's words, it was one Sunday night a few years later when the call came from her anxious daughter-in-law. Nancy's son, Ron, was distraught and talked of killing himself.

Nancy immediately called for a friend to drive her to her son's house. The situation was desperate. Nancy later told me about her son: "Ron voiced his despair, his weariness, his fears, and that he couldn't take it anymore. Nothing stopped the tormenting pain he was experiencing within. He was referring to his childhood memories and the bad relationship with his father that included abuse to him and his sister over and over again, and then her suicide—he never quite got over that. Things that happened to him in the army left a bad memory, his first marriage ended in divorce, and there were things he could not overcome that he felt caused heartache to others as well as himself. My heart ached for him. I was familiar with these tormenting feelings. He was unable to see any hope."

Nancy and her daughter-in-law talked to Ron into the early hours of the morning, assuring him of their love and understanding, of God's love and forgiveness for his past, and of hope. They finally felt that love had won out. Ron prayed with them, talking to God, directly, straightforwardly, asking his forgiveness, and that he be the Lord of his life. Nancy prayed too, thanking God for her son and committing Ron into God's keeping. "All of us had peace," she told me later over the phone. They all slept and then awoke Ron so he could get to work on time very early in the morning. Nancy and her daughter-in-law lay down again, only to be jolted awake by pounding on the door. It was a police officer. He would reveal nothing, only that they were to come with him. They were driven to Nancy's former husband's home. Nancy's daughter-in-law said, "Mom, there are police and barricades everywhere."

"I learned then that there are blessings in blindness," Nancy told me. "We had to inform the officers that my son was probably armed, suicidal, and an excellent marksman. When we were told that there was a body in the backyard, we assured them we felt it was Ron, but they were not convinced and had us talk on the PA system. I thank God I was unaware of all the people standing around, the news reporters, and the TV cameras. Less than an hour later, the police decided to close in, and that was hard. While we believed Ron was dead, we knew if he wasn't and didn't surrender, he would, in all probability, be shot."

Not only was Nancy's son found, but so was his father. It was a murder-suicide. Nancy does not speculate on what may have happened. God had given her a promise five years earlier that all her children would come to him, and when she talked to me the day after this incident, she was calm and confident. "God doesn't always answer our prayers in our preconceived way," she said. "The Bible speaks of sorrow as being refining. I have been in the refiner's fire," she could say later, adding, "and I have grown." She stood strong in the Lord, never wavering. Death is a wound to the living, and this family was deeply wounded. But wounds are meant to heal and, given time, they did heal. The natural response to death is grief and tears. Nancy and her family both grieved and cried. It became a part of the healing process.

God doesn't hand out medals to those who do not mourn and weep. Once again we were all reminded that Jesus didn't say we shouldn't mourn, but rather that we would, and that we would be blessed and comforted (Matt. 5:4).

Yes, God is a refiner but not an arsonist. The prophet Isaiah said it so well: "When you pass through the waters, I will be with you; and through the rivers, they shall not overflow you. When you walk through the fire, you shall not be burned, nor shall the flame scorch you. For I am the Lord your God . . . and I have loved you" (Isa. 43:2–4 NKJV).

Nancy's mother told me that during the last ordeal, in the loss of their grandson, God gave her this verse: "My grace is sufficient for you, for My strength is made perfect in weakness" (2 Cor. 12:9 NKJV). We should all remember those words.

❀ 5 ❀

Be Aware of Suicidal Gesturing

Take every threat of suicide seriously. Most people who are
suicidal are intensely suicidal only for a short period of time,
and this is usually in reaction to a specific newly introduced
stress or rejection. The suicidal crisis may last only for a few
hours, and if the victim can survive during this period of time
he may never be suicidal again.[1]

Dr. Paul Pretzel, *Understanding
and Counseling the Suicidal Person*

Suicide is generally perceptible, predictable, and prevent-
able. Some gestures, or signals, especially common to the
depressed person include the following: (1) Sleeplessness
or excessive sleeping. Sleeping is one way to cop out of the
raw realities of one's situation. (2) Loss of appetite or excessive
eating. There may also be a loss of interest in sexual activity.
(3) Languor—a general lethargy, loss of ambition, lack of interest, and an inability to concentrate. There is little aliveness

or alertness, and often there is unexplained crying. (4) Guilt and discouragement—much self-remorse and self-deprecation. The person indicates that all is hopeless.

Other signals of depression are as follows: (1) Withdrawal into isolation. This can occur even within the intimacy of the family. (2) Outright threats to commit suicide. (3) Writing a will and getting business in order. (4) Making a point of saying "Good-bye," "If I see you again," or "You won't have to be bothered with me much longer." (5) Giving away possessions. (6) Any *significant* change in personality or behavior. (7) Consulting with a physician, psychiatrist, or minister. (8) A sharp slump in academic or job performance. (9) Recent traumatic events. (10) Feelings of being unwanted and the idea that "My family would be better off without me."

Suicidal behavior, however, has a multiplicity of motivations. It can best be understood in terms of the actual person who was or is suicidal. Careful investigation after a suicide and conversations with loved ones and friends often reveal many clear attempts at communication that were missed, ignored, or misinterpreted by those closest to the suicide. Why, when the communications are so clear in retrospect, are they not received at the time they are given?

One possible answer is that we all have psychological defenses that can go into operation without our really being aware of it. Who wants to admit that someone they love is feeling suicidal?

Another answer is that we convince ourselves suicidal individuals are only trying to get sympathy or gain some attention or make us feel sorry for them; we don't believe they really mean what they are saying. Perhaps they have cried wolf on previous occasions, and this cry came to be regarded as a way of manipulation, and those around them were desensitized to their cries. Veiled aggression may also be involved—the desire on the part of suicidal individuals to get even with someone who has hurt or disappointed them, so they attempt to hurt themselves and then hope for sympathy.

Often such suicidal gestures are half-hearted attempts to kill themselves—just enough pills so that they are found after making a telephone call to tell someone what they've done. Threats are regarded as a form of blackmail by which suicidal persons hope to intimidate the people around them and make them feel responsible for their condition or death should they succeed. These are possible contributing factors that help explain why suicidal communications are not taken seriously.

One teenager who had a friend who succeeded in killing himself expressed ambivalent feelings. She knew her friend had entertained thoughts of suicide off and on for two years; she even knew he'd written about it in a journal and, in particular, because he liked to write poems, that suicidal thoughts were in his poems. He shared the poems with her, and then they would talk about them. She recounted, "But as I got his poems, I noticed that a lot of them had to do with death. It scared me. I didn't know how to react to it. I took it seriously. I was so scared that he'd try something, I went through two years just being petrified. I talked to him about it. Like his poem about the ladder, where he said if he fell off who would care? And I said, 'Peter, I'd care.' I got the impression that he didn't care about living. . . . I don't think he ever thought of how much he'd hurt other people by dying."

She and another girl talked about his poems and being scared. "But when you're just living you tend to forget. And it's not good but it happens. I'm the kind of person that I get so tied up in life that I forget about death. . . . I don't think the teachers took his stuff too seriously. I think they thought it was his imagination. The teachers at school tend to give a mark and forget about it; they're not willing to become involved. . . .

"When I first heard that he'd killed himself, I didn't believe it. I couldn't believe that he would do that to us. I felt it was a betrayal, but yet I had the feeling that it was coming because of his poems. I knew that it could happen so I wasn't surprised when it did. But I was hurt."[2]

You can sense the ambivalence. Suicidal gesturing was all through his poems, yet no one—parents, teachers, friends—took him seriously, although two of his friends were scared. His father found him in the snow. Beside him was a shotgun. The side of his face and head were blown away. Around him the snow was red with blood. The father fell to his knees and crumpled over his dead son's body. "Oh, no, God, no. Not my boy. Why? Why?" In the boy's blue ski jacket was a small index card on which a note had been scrawled: "I have fought hard and the internal fight I had was hell. Look under my bed for the whole story."[3]

The answer to Peter's father's "Why?" was under his son's bed, where they found two packets containing two notebooks that contained poetry, a short story, and day-to-day reflections faithfully recorded in the year prior to his suicide. That was his legacy to the world. Nothing else remained.

From this account we can see that threats must be taken seriously. Suicidal people usually are suffering from tunnel vision—a limited focus; their minds are unable to furnish them with a complete picture of how to handle what they perceive as seemingly intolerable problems.

In the case of this young man, here was someone considered an all-around superior student, trustworthy, dedicated, academically brilliant, deeply concerned with and unusually well informed on world problems, a good athlete, friendly, cheerful, conscientious. He had an intellect and vision of life far beyond his age. Could it be that he was too sensitive and introspective? "Death is worth dying to get away from life," he wrote. "Like when you look at all the evil that man has done to the world."

One wishes his mother had been a snoop, that she had found a farewell letter he wrote over a year before his suicide. The six things young Peter named in this letter as reasons for taking his life square in some respects with what researchers and psychologists point to as the answer to the question "Why?": (1) He was curious as to what happens after death. (2) Everyone was going to die sooner or later by old age or an atomic war, so why not sooner? (3) The pressure of schoolwork and homework was just too much. (4) He didn't feel his relationship with his parents was very good. (5) He saw the world turning into an evil place—too much corruption, exploitation, misery, and pain. (6) He felt he was really "screwed up in so many ways. [He had] so many questions about life and no answers. It really got to [him]."[4]

Suicide Contagion

The increasing number of suicides among young adults has called attention to a sort of suicide contagion. A ripple effect. To a young person's peers, suicide may look tragically heroic rather than simply tragic. In Peter's case, however, his friends, for the most part, felt what he had done was really stupid. One friend said, "He didn't accomplish a thing with his death, except to hurt people who were close to him."[5] None of these friends expressed the desire to join Peter in death. In fact, several of them viewed the suicide as a cop-out.

The Language of Behavior

Suicidal persons are very often starved for love. There may be a lot of instability within their relationships. Perhaps family members are feuding—one's parents or siblings. Or a husband and wife may be having difficulty in their marital relationship. Sometimes marital infidelity is involved, and the hurt and embarrassment are more than they can handle. There may be loss of community, of having familiar friends around. Our geographical mobility has contributed to social isolation, and this contributes to feelings of rootlessness and alienation.

Other factors contributing to suicide are the collision of genetic vulnerability (depression historically runs in the family) and poor early environment, which makes depression and feelings of despair predictable. There may be a history of childhood abuse and torment (as with my friend Nancy's two children). Traumatic events can trigger a bout with depression leading to suicide—separations (of parents or from one's mate), divorce, the breakup of a romance, loss of a job, inability to find employment, bankruptcy, the death of someone close. Any of these things can precipitate a suicide crisis, and listening to the language of behavior is strategic in preventing suicide.

Dr. Calvin J. Frederick, psychologist with the National Institute of Mental Health (NIMH), believed that suicidal persons often have ineffectual father-son, mother-daughter relationships. Individuals can suffer great pressure by trying to live up to parental expectations, and this carries over into adulthood. It was his belief that sons and daughters from broken homes were especially vulnerable. With the divorce rate in this country now exceeding over 50 percent of all marriages, this poses some serious problems. Certainly it should say to parents that they always need to be sensitive and aware.

I do not mean to imply that all children of divorce will exhibit signs of severe depression that can trigger suicidal thoughts. I simply mean to alert you to potential problems and how each of us needs to be sensitive to the need to help others through a temporary inability to cope.

Dr. Karl Menninger, in his book *Man Against Himself*, explains this: "Anyone who has sat by the bedside of a patient dying from a self-inflicted wound and listened to pleadings that the physician save his life, the destruction of which had only a few hours or minutes before been attempted, must be impressed by the paradox that one who has wished to kill himself does not wish to die."[6]

Primary Prevention

If you notice suicidal gesturing in anyone, the first and most important rule is to do something. Get help. Never assume that the crisis is over just because the person says it is or seems to feel and act more like his or her normal self.

Give friendship, love, and acceptance; show that you care. Communicate. Get the suicidal person to talk. Encourage expression of feelings. Accentuate the positive aspects of living. Remind the person of those who would be left behind, bereaved, saddened, and hurt, if he or she carried out this plan.

Don't make moral judgments. Concentrate on talking about things that will give him or her a reason and a will to live.

Don't get involved in life versus death arguments. Your goal should be to restore the person's feelings of self-worth and dignity.

Act. Take charge. Take pills away; take a gun away—whatever lethal weapons the person may be threatening to use. Involve the immediate help of others.

Secondary Intervention

I said it before, but it needs repeating: suicidal behavior can be understood as a manifestation of the person's need for some basic change in his or her life. Parents or the person's mate stand in a unique position to help. Sometimes what the suicidal person wants is not feasible (a dead husband, wife, or child cannot be revived; a broken love relationship cannot always be restored; a lost job cannot be retrieved), but efforts must be made to create some kind of support plan that will provide the suicidal person with a measure of security and hope for the immediate future.

The help of counselors trained in treating suicidal individuals is an essential part of recovery. Never minimize the need for such help. Whatever you can do, spare no effort to reach out to those persons whose suicidal gesturing should be interpreted as a cry for help. And don't hesitate to put your arms around them, hugging them, telling them you believe in them and love them. Touch is so important. Get them the help they need if it is at all within your means to do so.

It has been shown that even though suicidal persons may be alienated from whatever religious background they have had, organized religion has been able to work effectively in the area of suicide prevention. A report from the National Institute of Mental Health, "Action for Mental Health," indicates that more people initially take their emotional problems to clergy than to any other single professional group.

Oftentimes people seeking such help will veil or disguise their suicidal thoughts, but today's clergy, generally, are trained to read and interpret the communication these people are attempting to make. If there are clergy reading this who have not received such training, they should learn what they can through professional crisis facilities and organizations in their communities. Pastoral help is extremely important, and I hope the material in this book will be helpful to clergy. When dealing with seriously suicidal people, professional consultation and support should always be considered an indispensable part of treatment.

In response to a *Christianity Today* report on suicide, a retired physician wrote a letter to the editor in which he related that he'd had many years' experience as a medical examiner, which required his investigation into many suicides. He explained that clinical depression is a medical problem, and while support from pastors, families, friends, and counselors is useful, expert medical care is essential. He emphasized that pastors should prepare themselves by being personally acquainted with a reliable Christian physician or clinic known for expertise in this field. Then if a person comes to him or her with symptoms or signs of depression, and especially with a hint or threat of suicide, the pastor should contact the doctor or clinic personally. Moreover, this physician stressed that if it is an apparent emergency, pastors themselves should transport the depressed person for help. He also related that he himself had survived a serious clinical depression many years ago, so he was writing as not only a physician, but also a survivor of that kind of depression.[7]

If you or someone you know is suffering from clinical depression, read the book *Finding Your Way through Depression* by Pam Rosewell Moore. Pam, a beautiful Christian, was finally diagnosed with clinical depression after years of struggling with this problem. She asked the questions so many ask: "What about the gospel? Was I not disappointing the Lord Jesus Christ? Where was the joyful Christian I had once been? What was happening to me?"[8]

These questions surface when Christians confront the reality that they are clinically depressed. Because of those very questions, misconceptions about God's sovereignty (his right to direct an individual's life according to his plan), and a lack of understanding about depression itself, many Christians suffer needlessly just as Pam did. (See appendix C for a list of subtypes of depression.)

Archibald Hart points out how Christians struggle with acceptance of depression because they have been taught that God's servants are immune to depression, that if they have real faith they will never get depressed. So that means that if you are depressed, it is because you are spiritually inferior. "What a pack of downright lies!" Hart exclaims. "Yet many have come to believe it. I shudder when I read or hear some prominent Christian leader or preacher claiming that depression is a sign 'that you lack faith.' More frequently, I hear some naïve preacher say that depression is the result of 'God turning His back on you' because you have 'let Him down' or sinned. This idea is supposed to 'lift your faith'!"[9]

The truth is that all of us suffer from the effects of sin in this imperfect world. Pain, suffering, despondency, and depression happen. God in his sovereignty hasn't chosen to deliver his children from these effects; he gives us freedom of choice to make decisions that may indeed cause us some depression. It rains on the just and the unjust (see Matt. 5:45). Jesus himself said it. Bad things happen to good people, to God's people as well.

While we do not always understand pain and suffering, they are realities allowed by God, and they can and should draw us closer to him. The alternative is to blame God and suffer other consequences—loss of peace and unresolved anger.

Time can become our teacher. The school of life, the university of pain—whatever one wishes to call it, the lessons come in time as we allow God, the great Tutor, to teach us what he wants us to know as we respond in faith, believing that what he wills is for our ultimate best good. "I will instruct you (says the Lord) and guide you along the best pathway for your life; I will advise you and watch your progress" (Ps. 32:8).

❧ 6 ❧

Women and Suicide

Most of the 500,000 people who attempt suicide every year in America do not so much choose death as stumble down into it from a steep slope of despair.[1]

Lewis B. Smedes

The increase in female suicides has, in recent years, caused sociologists and mental health professionals some puzzlement. Males complete suicide at a rate four times that of females. However, females attempt suicide three times more often than males. These are the findings of the American Association of Suicidology.

Statistics from reporting organizations vary, and they do not always coincide relative to yearly reporting. The late Dr. Lewis Smedes's quote above shows five hundred thousand attempted suicides annually, yet many suicide attempts are never reported. These are probably, at best, guesstimates; if a medical doctor, professional person, or the law hasn't been called, the likelihood of an attempt getting recorded is slim. What statistics do reveal, however, is the alarming and sad fact that there is much unhappiness and a host of other disturbing emotions among people who decide to give up on life.

For women, the late forties and early fifties provide the greatest number of suicidal fatalities. Men characteristically employ more deadly means than women and appear to be less undecided about wanting to die when they are in a suicidal crisis.

Difficult Love Relationships

Nancy, whose story I shared in chapter 3, saw herself as deficient in the eyes of her husband and parents, and the thought of adding to her children's problems tipped the scale.

Many psychiatrists share the view that for divorced and discarded women, suicide is an effort to thwart loss of love by a husband or lover. This threatened or actual loss of love awakens childhood anxiety, with resultant feelings of hopelessness, guilt, and rage. Nancy fit that pattern. Suicide seeds are often planted in the minds of women who have difficult love relationships before the specific stimulus of a severed relationship occurs. My research has revealed that in many women the dynamics of suicide can stem from early childhood, when the foundation is laid for feelings about oneself. Often these women see themselves as victims of an unjust, severely distant, and deprived childhood. The deprivation has much to do with their relationships with parents with whom they suffer feelings of isolation, condemnation, and abandonment. As a result, early in life they acquire feelings of unworthiness and guilt for not fulfilling their parents' expectations. Low self-esteem leads to frustration, feelings of helplessness, and longings to express their feelings and desires but finding they are unable to do so. Some women who experience these things may harbor suicidal thoughts in their adult lives as they attempt to adapt to or compensate for their perceived deficiencies. These women's relationships with men run the danger of being obsessive, self-destructive, masochistic, and even sadistic. Divorce or abandonment usually result.

Strains of the Culture; Stress of Work

Between 1963 and 1976, when the national suicide rate for women went up by 45 percent, mental health professionals began to sit up and observe trends. What was happening? Why, for instance, in the city of Los Angeles, did the rate of suicide among women in the fifteen-to-thirty age group increase over 600 percent? At that time the California State Department of Public Health reported that the stresses and strains of "liberation" and work were driving more California women to suicide.

An article in *McCalls* magazine at that time reported that women were becoming more involved outside the family and were increasingly entering the work arena. Their drive for success and recognition increased pressures and opened more possibilities for failure.[2] It was very interesting that precisely in those areas where liberated women were making the most progress, the male-female suicide ratio moved toward equality.

There has been a dramatic increase in completed suicides by professional women. These are women who have achieved success in their chosen professions—medicine, psychology, writing, teaching, the arts, etc. Some helpful insights as to why can be found in the research and writings of psychoanalysts who seek to show the connection between women in the professional workplace and their encounters with men who really don't want to recognize women's expertise, leadership, and decision-making skills.

Another strong factor relates to the need for women to act decisively in their job roles. Translate that learned ability to act and to make decisions and stick to them in their professions into their personal lives, and you can see the problems this decisiveness poses when these women are confronted with personal challenges or some trauma.

Disappointment in Marriage

But it is not only the women working outside the home who make suicide attempts. According to Earl Grollman, who was long involved in family counseling in the state of Massachusetts, the bored housewife has the greatest suicide potential.[3] A woman approaches marriage with high expectations—expectations, unfortunately, that are all too often dashed on the cutting edge of the realities that accompany the marriage relationship. It is not all romantic evenings with candlelight dinners for two. Many young couples approach marriage totally unprepared for the inevitable challenges that arise, challenges that can turn into huge problems if not handled wisely. Often such couples need counseling, and often one (or both) of them is not prepared to admit they need help. Sometimes financial pressures make getting such help or going to marriage seminars impossible. Wise are churches that regard the ministry to married couples as a priority and provide counseling or opportunities for seminars at no cost. Wise too are those churches that recognize the importance of reading and making available resources (books, tapes, videos) that can help struggling couples (or individuals).

Every suicide or potential suicide has its own history, of course, but the disillusionment that shatters many women's dreams comes at the point of marriage adjustments. One young woman, hovering on the brink of a suicide attempt, wrote her younger brother a heart-wrenching letter. I include it here because I want you to see what faithfulness to God—trusting him, relying on his promises in the Bible, praying, and sticking it out—brought about. Here's the original letter:

It's been pretty hilly for me—there have been some valleys I've had to climb out of. In some of those valleys I put my foot in the wrong place and fell back again further than where I was before. . . .

Things are somewhat better now, and I shouldn't be writing a letter when I'm down; the trouble is I'm down most of the time and I know you are expecting a letter.

Steve [not his real name] has me worried. Three nights last week he stayed out until after midnight. . . . Somehow I muddled through last week but my memory of what happened is just a blur of hurt and frustration. Now it's like a bad dream, but I know it was real. Too real.

Steve doesn't know what he wants; he doesn't even know if he wants me. He doesn't like the responsibility that goes with marriage. I can't pressure him because then he screams, "Freedom!" He resents the fact that I have a relationship with God. He's turned his back on God. That's not going over too well with God!

At times when I am able to think straight, I can see what the Lord is doing and a real peace comes over me. I honestly think I would have committed suicide by now if I didn't have the Lord to hold me up.

It's like when the Lord sees a wave coming my way, He lifts me up above it, just high enough so I still get wet enough to learn and to show me how blessed I really am that I didn't go all the way under. When I look down, it's like I see Steve

65

gasping for air and struggling, fighting all the way—and the whole time all he has to do is stop fighting and reach up for the Lord to pull him up too. Someday he may not be able to fight the wave hard enough and he may not come up again—then it will take an act of grace and mercy for the Lord to reach down and give him one more chance.

I've heard and read stories of other women who have gone through what I'm going through. I never thought I'd have to go through it though. Let me tell you, I'm learning a lot. Mostly I'm learning to just hang in there and to pray. I know I can't change things on my own. I keep praying and ask God to give me strength and patience in my dealings with Steve. The last time I prayed that, it was as though I heard God say, "You're doing fine . . ." That's neat, you know. I think I'm blowing it, but God says I'm doing fine. What would I do without God?

That marriage survived, and the couple has celebrated their twenty-fifth anniversary. The husband made a dramatic turn-about in his life, and together they established a Christian home. Their children were born and nurtured in the Bible and now, as young people, are living for the Lord. It took a commitment on the wife's part to remain true to her wedding vows, and it took unceasing prayer on her part and on the part of family members who knew what was happening and joined their prayers with hers. She never gave up, and not only her husband but also his friends turned their lives over to the Lord. This is as powerful a story as I've ever encountered, clearly showing how God himself will intervene, bless, honor, make right, restore, and take care of his children.

Another young wife told me she repeatedly hit her head against the wall in her bedroom in a vain attempt to injure herself so that she would die. Still another shared her frequent desire to get in the car and head for a certain section of the highway where there was a bridge abutment. "It would be so easy to speed up . . . ," she said, sad eyes betraying her pain as her voice trailed off. In each of these instances, my husband and I were able to help these women and their husbands. We thanked God that we were able to be intervenors.

The author of an article entitled "Suicide and Women" in a national women's magazine questioned why the suicide rate among young women was going up. She wondered if there was any way to find some sort of explanation of the particular causes. One can understand the poverty, isolation, and hopelessness that surrounds the elderly, but what is it that invades the lives of young women that causes them to respond with such a strong desire to die? This failure of the will to live is an indescribably overwhelming force that should not exist in the lives of those who really have so much for which to live.

It has been demonstrated that a certain area of the will functions in any suicide but that these deep pits of melancholy paralyze to such a degree that the resolution necessary to continue living is lacking for those who become completed suicides.

Fear of rejection plays a role in the agony of uncertainty young women experience as they see their husbands struggling with the frustrations that accompany the responsibilities of marriage and the maintenance of a home. Not only is this true for young married women, but the same anxiety exists among women who have been married for years. Much domestic violence has depression at its core. Often there is a lot of financial pressure, trying to keep up with the Joneses, or just maintenance of a standard of living to which they've become accustomed. Perhaps they haven't been able to save for their children's education, or they begin to worry about retirement. Bad investments may have intruded into their security.

In the final analysis, the mystery surrounding motive and mood remains shrouded in the death act itself. The problem is, you can't talk to the victim and are left with whatever remaining family members or others wish to divulge.

Crumbling Family Values

When women are caught in the crossfire of tangled marital relationships, with infidelity having reared its ugly head, the wife, if she is the victim in the affair, will sometimes take her own life. Such incidents show the terrible possible consequences when passion goes out of control. These things happen even among Christians and further point to the crumbling of family values.

Women Differ from Men

There are those who believe women are less sincere in their suicide attempts (that their attempts are attention getters more than anything else). I know of one woman whose attempts landed her in the hospital three times before she finally overdosed to such an extent that her family wasn't able to get there in time to rescue her. With each attempt, she took the pills and then phoned her sons or husband and told them what she'd done. She was considered a very narcissistic woman who was also extremely jealous and distrustful of her husband.

The facts reveal that most women do not really want to die at all, that they are not seriously thinking about being dead. They look upon a suicide attempt as a release, an escape from pain.

Women are also prone to look upon suicide as the right thing to do—to sacrifice themselves to spare their loved ones future problems and further anguish. Nancy's story is a case in point. The novelist Virginia Woolf left letters to her husband and sister, saying in the suicide's characteristic way, "I can't go on spoiling your life any longer." These women cast their suicides in a heroic mold—that's the way they want to be remembered. Women are more inclined to do that sort of thing than men. That statement is not meant to demean women but is a recognition of the emotional nature of the female.

Because the scenario of the ultimate desperation is scripted by each individual, it is unsafe to make generalizations about suicide victims. Many complex factors enter into the victim's decision. Recurrent depression that frequently triggers suicide can have a biochemical basis. Family histories show a predisposition to suicide. Causes of the despondency that precipitates suicide are tangled. Conviction on the part of the victim that his or her circumstances are unalterable will drive him or her to the act. Revenge is the motive for some suicides—women kill themselves for that reason more frequently than men. Personal anguish and the shame that accompanies the loss of love are more than many women can bear. To know that your husband or lover has left you for someone else is devastating. Life is for living, but for some the effort is too great.

Women may look at their offspring and see failure—failure in themselves as mothers. They know that others see the failure also. Self-hatred, self-accusation, and their limitations rise up to stare them in the face. They find this intolerable. They cannot face their own critical analysis nor the condemning finger of others. They can't deal with it.

Formidable hormonal changes can play havoc with women's moods and contribute to female depression (see also chapter 12). This was one of the problems Nancy experienced (see chapter 3). Dr. Archibald Hart writes about effective treatments for depression. His insights from a Christian psychologist's perspective are very enlightening. The biggest struggle, he says, is to find the right medication that relieves depression but has the fewest unpleasant side effects. What works for one may not work for another, but the important point he makes is that, male or female, one needs to work with one's doctor and be patient and cooperative. He explains that the discovery of the drug Prozac revolutionized treatment of depression, especially in women because of their unique type of depression, and opened up a whole new battery of medications called SSRIs (selective serotonin re-uptake inhibitors), which work mainly on serotonin. (Serotonin is one of the three major neurotransmitters in the brain that affect mood. The other two are norepinephrine and dopamine.) "Monthly and lifecycle variations in estrogen levels greatly influence the serotonin levels in the female brain."[4] There were many early attacks on medications by those opposed to all medications, but Hart calls them "really miracle drugs," and "a gift from God," which they certainly are to those for whom they are prescribed "who have once again found a life."

Suicide Methods Generally Used by Women

Suicide methods seem to vary by gender, with women selecting more passive means of killing themselves—sleeping pills, poisons, or gas. Women want to look their best in death, so they usually don't attempt to do something that would disfigure them. Nancy was an exception with her choice of a gun, but remember her concern about wearing the right dress?

Women want the painless way out, but although women statistically use passive methods more often than violent methods, it doesn't mean they never use guns or hang themselves. Depressed women should not be around guns any more than depressed men should be. It must be emphasized that women *do* use guns, and they *do* hang themselves. An editor friend told me of two women she personally knew, each of whom used hunting rifles, and one of her best friend's business partners hanged herself.

Nancy took sleeping pills in case she didn't die right away; she didn't want to lie there suffering. The easy availability of potentially dangerous drugs is offered as a factor in the increase in women's suicide rates. In the course of writing this book, I received a phone call from a woman telling me she had flushed all her Valium down the toilet while she was on vacation. "It was tempting me; I was despondent and the future looked so bleak. I knew if I kept those pills around I might take all of them without really meaning to. I do want to live, but it's just that I can't see the end from the beginning. Is there any hope?"

A Letter That Carried a Warning

Someone wrote to Ann Landers with a warning: "Prospective Suicides: Think of Those You'll Hurt." The letter read,

Dear Ann Landers: I am a fairly attractive woman in my middle forties. To the outside world I appear to have everything a woman could want—a lovely home, beautiful children, a successful husband, and I've even excelled in sports and won some trophies. No one would suspect that I've gone through periods of severe depression and about two years ago attempted suicide.

I have something important to say to the readers of your column who may have at any time contemplated taking their lives. The information I am about to pass along for free, cost me $3,000 in psychiatric bills. The next time you look longingly at that handgun, or that bottle of pills, or a bridge or window you believe will put an end to your agonies, remember the husband or wife or children or parents you would leave behind. No matter how blameless they may be, they will always think it was their fault that you killed yourself. All the rationalization in the world won't change it. They will carry to their graves the thought that something they did, or failed to do, caused you to take your life. Do you want to place such a burden on your loved ones? If you commit suicide you'll surely do it—Thank God I didn't.

Ann Landers responded with these words:

Dear Friend: The impact of any given letter is, of course, an unknown quantity, but I can tell you for certain that your letter prevented at least one suicide someplace in the world today. Thank you for writing it.[5]

✼7✼

Men and Suicide

We didn't talk about my father with each other, and we didn't talk about him outside the family either partly at least because suicide was looked on as something a little shabby and shameful in those days. Nice people weren't supposed to get mixed up with it.[1]

Frederick Buechner, *Telling Secrets*

Ask ten different people if they have ever contemplated suicide, and the very reticence of some to reply provides the clue that they have. During the course of writing this book, I asked a much-respected businessman if he thought a book on this subject was needed. His answer was an immediate yes, said in such a way that I felt there was more to his answer than he was relating.

"Shall we talk about this?" I said quietly as I regarded him.

"For many years now, I've held out to myself the idea that if things get too tough, I can always kill myself," he responded. "I know that comes as a shock, but since you asked, I want to be honest. Maybe it will help in the writing of the book; maybe it is a reflection of what lots of men think. If so, we are in trouble. Try and provide us with some reasons and answers as to why we feel that way and what we can do."

Early in my research I discovered what researchers describe as the most typical suicide. He is depicted as a well-adjusted mainstream American—a male in his forties, a breadwinner, a family man, a homeowner, and a man whose best years would seem to be ahead of him. In addition, researchers show that the suicidal male is always a person who has encountered problems—most often with his wife, with his family, or in other personal relationships—problems he feels he cannot cope with.

Firearms are the most common method of suicide used by men (74 percent). This helps explain why suicides among men have a tragic finality about them. Women, on the other hand, traditionally have chosen slow methods of death, such as ingestion of poisons and medicines, that increase the chance of rescue. Such attempts are generally interpreted as a woman's way of asking for help, of calling attention to her problems and asking others to be concerned about them. Men, however, often construe asking for help as weak and unmanly.

It is also felt that women tend to be more vain than men. And while this is probably true, men also notice the relentless march that moves them toward middle age. They experience physiological alterations (appearance and often agility) and accompanying psychological changes. They have not attained certain goals; and dreams, aspirations, and plans begin to appear as unlikely to be realized. Depression sets in—a deep-down, immobilizing despair that saps creative energy and drive. With this comes loss of a will to live. The tragedy is that the wish to die and loss of the will to live is usually transitory, and the suicide's depression has temporarily blinded him to other ways out of his dilemma. If family members or business associates were only aware, and if when the person feels suicidal he would reach out and confide in someone and seek some help, all it would take is a word of encouragement and understanding to make such a person conscious of alternative solutions to his situational difficulty.

Male Depression

Hart's book *Unmasking Male Depression* is the best material I have read on the subject of male depression, which Hart calls "the great cover-up" contributing to the high incidence of completed suicide among men. "Depression is a disease with devastating consequences," he writes. He points to an article in the *American Journal of Psychiatry* that says men are four to six times more likely to commit suicide than are women. "What's the connection?" Hart asks. "Suicide is largely a depression problem. Why would men have such a high rate of suicide if it wasn't because they are depressed? You don't kill yourself just because you are bored! Yet close loved ones often attribute it to moodiness or a personality flaw. Fathers often pass on from generation to generation the denial of depression by excusing any mood deviation with a sweeping, 'I used to be like that, so he'll grow out of it also.'" Hart explains that the generally accepted understanding is that real men never get depressed!

The fact is that real men do suffer from depression. Authentic men, not just milquetoasts, wimps, and nerds. Television news icon Mike Wallace had it. Novelist William Styron had it. Both went public and spoke about their experiences with severe depression. Some Christians like to point to such experiences as a secular problem. Emphatically no, says Hart. Scores of Christian men also suffer from depression. He points to some great Christian men who all knew about serious depression firsthand: John Wesley, Charles Spurgeon, John Calvin, and Martin Luther. Besides being famous, these men also transcended bouts with depression: Abraham Lincoln, Winston Churchill, Martin Luther King, and Nelson Mandela. "Depression is a common theme among great men in general, believe it or not," writes Hart. In addition to those already mentioned, these also suffered from depression: Goethe, Bismarck, Tolstoy, Robert E. Lee, and scores of authors and poets. The encouraging word to any man suffering from depression is that you keep company with some of the greatest human beings who have ever lived.[2]

Statistics Tell a Story

Suicide statistics about men tell a troubling story. Consider the following:

- Eighty percent of all suicides in the United States are men.
- The male suicide rate at midlife is three times higher than at any other time; for men over sixty-five, it is seven times higher.
- Twenty million American men will experience depression sometime in their life.
- Sixty to eighty percent of depressed adults never get professional help, and men are at the top of the list.
- It can take up to ten years and exposure to at least three mental health professionals to properly diagnose this disorder.

- Eighty to ninety percent of men seeking treatment can get relief from their symptoms.[3]

Frederick Buechner, celebrated author of many works of fiction and nonfiction, was ten years old when his father turned on the engine of the family Chevy and sat down on the running board to wait for the exhaust to kill him. He describes this as a time when *suicide* was indeed the whispered word:

> There was no funeral to mark his death and put a period at the end of the sentence that had been his life, and as far as I can remember, once he had died, my mother, brother, and I rarely talked about him much ever again, either to each other or to anybody else. It made my mother too sad to talk about him, and since there was already more than enough sadness to go round, my brother and I avoided the subject with her as she avoided it for her own reasons also with us. Once in a while she would bring it up but only in very oblique ways. I remember her saying things like . . . "Now things are going to be different for all of us." . . . His suicide was a secret we nonetheless tried to keep as best we could, and after a while my father himself became such a secret.[4]

Buechner wrote a novel called *The Return of Ansel Gibbs* twenty-two years later. In it he told a brief and fictionalized version of his father's death, and the most accurate word he could find to describe his mother's reaction to this novel was *fury*. He was in his fifties and his mother in her eighties before he dared write on "the forbidden subject" again. It was an autobiographical book called *The Sacred Journey*, and in it he made no reference to his mother. He felt sure she never read it. Still later, after his mother's death, he wrote a novel called *Godric*, in which, once again, the suicide of his father plays an important role. This was forty-four years after his father's death.

Buechner was painfully honest about his reasons for writing so often about this event in his life:

> I was writing more than I had known I knew with the result that the book was not only a word *from* me—my words painstakingly chosen and arranged into sentences by me alone—but also a word out of such a deep and secret part of who I am that it seemed also a word to me.[5]

He also wrote *The Wizard's Tide*, telling the story of his father's death the way it should be told to a child: "In other words the way I need to tell it to the child who lives on inside me as the children we were lives on inside all of us. . . . By telling it in language a child could understand, I told it as the child who I both was in 1936 and still am in 1990. I relived it for that child and *as* that child with the difference that this time I was able to live it right."[6]

Including his book *Telling Secrets*, from which these quotes were gleaned, Buechner has written five books relating the event of and his reaction to his father's suicide. In short, the suicide had a major impact upon his young life that carried on in one way or another throughout his life. When he speaks of his father's exodus from this life, he refers to it as "an escape from bondage." He explains that he has talked about this because he believes readers will recognize themselves or people they have known and loved in what he relates. "We all have stories to tell—where we have come from and the people we have met along the way—and God has his way of making himself known to each of us powerfully and personally."[7]

I have included Buechner's story because of the healing of the child in him that took place as he allowed his memory to help him work through all that had happened and because of his hope that it could help others who have been wounded by life experiences that happened to them long ago. These things will always remain a part of who we are, he explains, just as the glad and gracious things will too. "Even the saddest things can become, once we have made peace with them, a source of wisdom and strength for the journey that still lies ahead."[8]

Reclaiming one's own life and coming to grips with what may have happened to a loved one, perhaps a father, a husband, a brother, a lover, a friend or acquaintance—how needful it is, and how important to know that God is always there offering possibilities of healing and hope for the future.

Executive Suicides among Males

The pattern of executive suicide looks like this: A rising young executive, aflame with creative ideas, moves through a series of regular promotions. Then, in what should be highly productive middle years, he suddenly "flames out." As the executive reaches the crest of life, he begins to struggle with the inevitability of his own death. He has to revise his life goals in terms of what is still possible to do. He has to be realistic and settle for a little less than he had hoped to achieve. For the man who is not reaching the goals he has set for himself, the effects can be unsettling or even devastating. The tragedy is that in this country, for years we have perpetuated a "youth cult." We seem to worship at the shrine of youth. Men who are coming into what could be their greatest potential are often stripped of their positions and replaced by younger people. That is wrong. A plea to business and industry is in order. When a man has proven himself competent and has been loyal, to deny him future progression in a company merely because the company is looking for new, young blood is a cruel recourse that can lead to serious consequences.

The rigid demands that so many men place upon themselves is neither wise nor fair, neither to themselves nor to their families. Some self-appraisal is called for. The economic needs of families today propel many men into long hours of fatiguing work, with accompanying pressures for achievement and approval forced upon them. Husbands and wives need to communicate to each other their values. It is one thing for a man to have high aspirations, but it is another thing to be so driven by the need to fulfill these goals that his wife and family feel excluded from his life. Success for success's sake is not right motivation. Such a man is a prime target for suicidal thoughts when business reversals rear their ugly heads, or when he is overtaken by fatigue, or when he finds himself resorting to the use of alcohol or drugs.

A woman wrote Ann Landers explaining that her husband was an executive who took an overdose of sleeping pills and ended his misery. He wasn't trying to punish anyone—they had a good relationship. She wrote, "He had overwhelming, insoluble financial problems. He felt defeated, helpless, disgraced and was too tired to keep fighting. He tried so hard to make it—but he couldn't. . . . My husband loved me very much. But being a success in business meant more to him than anything in the world and there was nothing I could do about it." She signed her letter "At Peace."

British poet-critic A. Alvarez, in *The Savage God*, spoke of suicide theory and statistics as being quite unilluminating. He spoke of the "shabby, confused, agonized crisis which is the common reality of suicide." [9]

Recession and Suicide

In times of recession the suicide rate always rises. The much-loved, award-winning poet Helen Steiner Rice, rightly called the "Ambassador of Sunshine," lost her husband to the crash when the stock market plummeted in October 1929 and the Great Depression of 1931–32 followed. He took his own life, overcome by melancholy, having sunk into the pit of despair, with the loss not only of all his assets but, worse, of his pride. Franklin Rice was considered one of Dayton, Ohio's, foremost businessmen, having become a vice president of Dayton Savings and Trust Company, overseeing its trust functions. He was also considered one of the city's most eligible bachelors at the time he and Helen met. But Helen herself was already a nationally known lecturer and writer. Their Caribbean honeymoon was a dream come true, and when they began their married life in the spring of 1929, it seemed a storybook beginning. A lifetime of luxury and wedded bliss appeared to stretch before them. Helen entered a world of opulence the likes of which she had never experienced before, but for whatever reason, it made her uneasy.

Helen was a very optimistic, enthusiastic, persevering person by nature, and she knew that the financial crisis brought on by the stock-market crash was no time to abandon her beliefs. She was confident that in time she and Franklin could overcome the obstacles fate placed before them. She drew on her past success and was offered a fine position with the Gibson Art Company, who asked her to move from Dayton to Cincinnati. It was obvious that the Great Depression was not a short-lived problem. Still, Franklin resisted the idea of a permanent move. She asked herself how she could save her husband's pride and pay their bills at the same time. After weighing her options, she decided that her husband's pride would have to take a backseat to survival, so she took up residence in a downtown Cincinnati hotel, and her husband drove up to get her so they could spend weekends together in their Dayton home. Franklin was deeply hurt over his financial reversals, realizing that the crash was a disaster far beyond his comprehension. His bank's assets, as well as his own, had disappeared, and the couple was deeply in debt. Unable to find a suitable job and unable to contend any longer with the strain of his circumstances, Franklin Rice drove his car into the garage, closed the door, and breathed in the carbon monoxide fumes. It was October 10, 1932.

It was an unimaginably painful time for Helen, and she struggled to find clues that would help her understand the meaning behind this unexpected loss. She gradually mustered the strength to confront both the emotional and financial turmoil occasioned by her husband's death. It wasn't easy—far from it—but she was sustained by her faith in God, her fighting spirit, and a memory of the Franklin Rice who had sat with her on top of the world for a few months during their brief married life. As the hurt eased, Helen realized that her pain was not an enemy to be feared but a blessing that made her more aware of the dimensions of human suffering. Her poems, greeting cards, and books reflect that indomitable spirit and are still bringing hope and healing to millions worldwide.[10]

The Franklin Rice suicide was repeated across the country in cities as well as small towns. With the collapse on Wall Street, the whole debt structure came tumbling down. The economy sputtered to a halt. Newspapers were full of the tragic stories of men jumping from buildings and killing themselves in various ways. Eddie Cantor, the Broadway comedian, added a joke to his routine in which he would tell of a hotel reservations clerk asking a guest, "Do you want the room for sleeping or for jumping?"

Depression Fallout in the Heartland

I was a Depression-era baby. My father died of cancer five months before I was born. Everything he had saved and planned for his wife and children was wiped out in the bank closing in our small Iowa town. The aftermath of the Depression impacted our family in that now Mother had to go to work to support her three fatherless children. I remember, among other things, having to cut out cardboard to put in the soles of my school shoes. Those were tough times. Mother survived by working very hard, but I recall the hushed talk of a suicide that occurred in a home near where we lived. I was a young child, but I remember that terrible tragedy and its aftermath in that farming community.

More and more men react to a single defeat in business or some kind of financial setback by becoming suicidal. Generally these are men who have been very successful, as their top-ranking positions indicate, and also men who have strong consciences. To attempt suicide is to act in violation of their consciences, yet they are so desperate that they do it anyway. A double tragedy. These are men who are needed in society, men whose families feel the loss deeply.

When status is destroyed, when self-esteem is shaken to the very core and the future is unpredictable, with no solution in sight, a man's perspective gets out of focus. He begins to think irrationally. Researchers tell us that if such a man has sustained psychological bruises in childhood, has experienced the loss of love and support (through death, divorce, or separation from parents), he may have developed deeply ingrained habit patterns of ego ideal aspirations. The consequent pressures to achieve perfection, with the threat of real or imagined failure, may drive him to attack himself in the form of accidents or, in the extreme, to commit suicide.

This form of self-flagellation is not uncommon. A lifetime of competitive living and being burdened by the threat of failure explains to a large degree why men resort to suicide. Again we see the loss of hope where a person is overwhelmed by a sense of futility.

Farmers: Bankruptcies, Staggering Indebtedness, and Loss of Hope

A feature story in the *San Jose Mercury News* caught my attention when we lived in California's Silicon Valley. It told the story of a 63-year-old Iowa farmer succumbing to debt and hard times who snapped in a way that is hard to understand. He was considered a good man by his family, his neighbors, and local people, including the police. Everyone was hard put to fathom what he did. He took a twelve-gauge shotgun and shot the president of the bank to which he was indebted, a neighbor with whom he had quarreled, then his wife, and finally himself. "[The] cause of all the deaths, everyone said, was the farm crisis. . . . If there were an Arlington National Cemetery for farmers felled by high interest rates and low prospects, [this man] would be buried in it. So says everyone."[11]

The reporter stated, "The conventional wisdom about conventional wisdom is that there is usually something to it. In this case, common sense tells you that a 63-year-old man, facing bankruptcy and staggering indebtedness, out of cash and out of hope, could simply go crazy. Common sense tells you also that hard times could not be the entire answer. Other farmers, some of them much worse off, have done nothing remotely similar. Once again, we are humbled by how much we do not know."[12]

This was a desperate farmer, driven by the specter of poverty, "a hard-working entrepreneur, up against nature, the bank and the vagaries of traders in places like Chicago." He was an honest man, thrifty, "the embodiment of almost every American virtue—self-employed, self-reliant and God-fearing. . . . Hard times kill: on the farm *and* in the ghetto."[13]

Ill Health, Drugs, Alcohol, and Suicide

People who have a low pain threshold are particularly vulnerable to depression. Such persons may be using prescribed medications. It is no secret that the easy availability of drugs has brought out suicidal tendencies that might otherwise have remained latent.

The Yale University School of Medicine studied 258 men and women following unsuccessful suicide attempts. They discovered a marked disparity between the seriousness of the intent to commit suicide and the medical complications when an attempt failed. Interviews with the 53 patients who attempted violent methods (wrist cutting, shooting, hanging) showed that the people who used these methods were more intent on killing themselves than the 205 who took pills. Interestingly enough, the medical effects were considerably less for violent attempters. Only 63 percent needed medical attention, compared to 92 percent of the pill poppers. Pill ingestors also tended to be younger—53 percent were under age twenty-six compared with only 33 percent of those who used knives, ropes, and guns. Researchers point out that what this reveals is an ignorance of the potential lethality of medications in these young attempters.[14]

85

Sleeplessness brought on by depression will often send a person to the doctor seeking relief. In a moment of desperation, the individual may take all the sleeping pills. And I recall only too well that this is what I did.

Clinical Depression: The Feeling of Being "Scooped Out"

J. B. Phillips, esteemed British translator (*The New Testament in Modern English*) and prolific author of many best-selling books, revealed in his autobiography, *The Price of Success*, that without any warning the springs of his creativity were suddenly dried up, and the ability to communicate disappeared overnight. He suffered a severe clinical depression that lasted for several years. One doctor told him he was "scooped out." He had never heard of the word *depression* used in a technical sense and didn't even know there was such a thing. He took a few days off, canceled a few engagements, and tried to take things easy.

> But it didn't work, the feeling of being drained of all emotion and desire persisted and I simply ceased to work. . . . After a few months, during which I was not entirely idle, I found the mental pain more than I felt I could bear and I went as a voluntary patient to a psychiatric clinic. . . . That was the point of breakdown. . . . It may help [others] to know that one whom the world would regard as successful and whose worldly needs are comfortably met can still enter this particular hell, and have to endure it for quite a long time.[15]

While writing this book, I shared with a friend what I was working on. When I told her about J. B. Phillips, she identified immediately. "I've been there," she stated. "I suffered through clinical depression for two years. What Phillips related in his book is so true."

Phillips explained that the "nameless mental pain" he endured was "so overwhelming that one can understand the temptation to suicide." He said he was not talking about actual mental disease or insanity, but

> of those intense pressures which build up, possibly for years, and result in the often quite unexpected collapse of a personality. . . . Even today with all the advances in medical and psychiatric treatment there is a vast amount of ignorance even among the so-called experts. Such an attack or series of attacks might last for weeks, months or even years and then vanish without a trace. I can only testify to the fact that it would have been of inestimable comfort and encouragement to me in some of my darkest hours if I could have come across even one book written by someone who had experienced and survived the hellish torments of mind which can be produced. And, alas, I know very few clergy or ministers who would even know what the sufferer was talking about.[16]

And he adds, "That is why I decided, however reluctantly, that this chapter [in his book] must be written by someone who has experienced the almost unendurable sense of terror and alienation."[17]

Physical manifestations of ill health will often force a person, a man in particular, to think of ending it all. When degenerative diseases set in, there are those who cannot cope with confinement to bed. But the sudden eruption of irrational fear and nameless panic that accompanies mental pain also triggers suicidal thoughts.

Installment Plan Suicides

If a person has a drinking problem, there is always the potential danger of the combination of drugs with alcohol—a deadly twosome. People who find life intolerable and unmanageable often participate in what psychiatrists call "death-oriented behavior." Alcoholics fit that label. Why does a person drink? Usually drinking to excess is an attempt to drown one's sorrows, to block out the reality of one's difficult circumstances, to escape responsibility.

Oftentimes, people who live alone experience isolation, desolation, loneliness, anxiety, fear, and uncertainty. Lonely aloneness breeds a kind of despair and an unconscious desire to end it all. In time these individuals accomplish what they are unconsciously attempting to do—contributing to their own demise. Alcohol also deepens aggressiveness, which, when turned against oneself, may lead directly to a deliberate suicide attempt. Many of these attempts are successful, some because the individual has gotten behind the wheel of a car.

Autocide

One of the best places to look for disguised suicides is on the road—traffic fatalities. Why do we see so much road rage in today's society? Has someone ever shot around you on the highway going well beyond the safe driving limits and you say, "Wow, he's going to kill himself!"? Precisely. Or someone will dangerously weave in and out of traffic, endangering not only himself but innocent victims of his angry, irrational behavior. I have experienced this and to myself have cried out, "Oh my word. He is a menace to safety," and I have deliberately pulled into the slow lane and slowed my pace to get away from that kind of driver. Such drivers' desire to die may be a subconscious wish, but the Federal Center for Studies of Suicide Prevention, Bethesda, Maryland, and the Los Angeles Suicide Prevention Center can offer solid evidence that many otherwise inexplicable crashes are actually disguised suicides. Behavioral scientists, as well as police, investigating highway deaths, note such things as dry, straight roads, lack of skid marks, and a car smashed against a tree or a bridge abutment. The report may say "improper driving," but circumstantial evidence strongly supports autocide.

A University of California, San Diego, study paper analyzing traffic fatalities showed that the more publicity given to a suicide story, particularly when the suicides involved well-known people, the more the number of auto fatalities rose.[18]

An interesting statistic from the *New England Journal of Medicine* revealed that for ten years following the Vietnam War, veterans were up to 86 percent more likely to commit suicide than were their civilian peers. Moreover, 53 percent more were likely to die in motor-vehicle accidents.

One woman, a failed suicide, explained that her life had been a series of failures—including unsuccessful and prolonged periods of psychiatric treatment—and she voiced the concern that many "accidents" were actually carefully planned suicides by people who had no desire to live but wanted to spare their loved ones the guilt. "Thousands, I'll bet," she said.

Even while finishing this book, the news reported on the Jeep that had been parked on a railroad crossing near Glendale, California, by a man who had planned to remain in the car, thus killing himself by autocide. It caused two trains to collide causing the deaths of eleven people. At the last moment the man jumped from the vehicle. He is now being held on charges of murder for the deaths of the innocent victims. What a tragic story.

Suicide is a complex behavior usually caused by a combination of factors. The problems of this man so overwhelmed him that it led to this. Whether it's a diagnosable mental or substance abuse disorder or both, relationship problems, unemployment—whatever the cause—despair, depression, feelings of hopelessness, and self-loathing result and cause senseless heartache when suicide or failed suicide takes place.

Death Is a Robber

Death is a robber. That fact cannot be denied. But death by suicide brings the greatest affront to all who remain. Indeed, the death of someone by suicide is the robbing of a life in an untimely way. Most everyone would agree with J. B. Phillips, who called our world "bewildering." Indeed, our only hope is in God.

Also, while writing this book, I learned of two Christian professional men who killed themselves. One of these men was a pastor, the other a writer.

My prayer as I have written this difficult chapter is that you, the reader, by shoring yourself up with as much knowledge as possible—and, hopefully, this book is helping to do that—will be able to respond to those faced with crushing personal problems. We can be gatekeepers. (More on this in chapter 13.)

❧ 8 ❧

By Any Name, It's Tragic

Suicide is a fatal game that leads from lucidity in the face of existence to a flight from light.

Albert Camus

Those who die for their faith, their strong beliefs, or for a cause we call martyrs. Those who die in the line of duty, such as servicemen or policemen, we call heroes. Those who die saving others we call brave and selfless. And those who die by their own hand we call suicides. Self-murderers others might say.

Death before dishonor and suicide for love have been popular themes among poets and playwrights for centuries. On paper or on the stage, the suffering of a tragic hero or heroine who ends up taking his or her own life is often made to appear noble.

You may remember the news story when in Dallas, Texas, a high school student sequestered class members in the classroom, holding them all at gunpoint, and then allowed them to leave, with the exception of his ex-girlfriend and the teacher. At that point he turned the gun on himself while the ex-girlfriend and teacher had to stand by and watch. This lovelorn young man wanted the former girlfriend to suffer by remembering for the rest of her life what she had done by jilting him. It was another tragedy of monstrous proportions.

In actual life there is nothing grandiose about the act of suicide. It's been said that suicide is ugly for onlookers, devastating for relatives, and harrowing even for those professionally involved. Anyone who has been at all close to a suicidal situation knows it is impossible to come away remaining aloof and unfeeling.

We cannot even begin to imagine how the father of the minister of music at a church must have felt when he discovered his son's lifeless body hanging from the garage rafters. Love for another woman, with no way out of the tangled mess without disrupting his home and scandalizing the ministry, caused him to do the unthinkable in a moment of emotional insanity. I say "emotional insanity" because if he had been thinking rationally, he would have recognized that divorce was nothing in comparison to the atrocity of suicide he was contemplating committing against himself, his wife, his children, his parents, and the church.

The common denominator in most suicides is the threat of, or actual rupture of, a relationship. Usually it's the one being rejected who thinks he or she can't face the future alone, and so, feeling unloved and inadequate, he or she opts out.

Copping Out Rather than Coping

A midfifties woman I know discovered her husband's slumped body in the front seat of his car. He had rigged a way for the exhaust fumes to be piped into his car, thus copping out rather than coping with health problems that seemed insurmountable. His wife and three children were left to pick up the broken pieces of their lives and cope with the multitude of problems his copping out left.

Stories such as this, however, don't show the agony that precipitates the suicide act. And every suicide has its own history. Writer A. Alvarez, in telling of his own suicide attempt, explained, "Each sporadic burst of work, each minor success and disappointment, each moment of calm and relaxation, seemed merely a temporary halt on my steady descent through layer after layer of depression, like an elevator stopping for a moment on the way down to the basement. At no point was there any question of getting off or changing the direction of the journey."[1] Alvarez attempted suicide by swallowing forty-five pills on top of a good deal of alcohol.

The list of gifted, creative people who have killed themselves is long. Any such list is tragic. You may recognize some of these names: John Berryman, Anne Sexton, Hart Crane, Virginia Woolf, Sylvia Plath, Ernest Hemingway, Marilyn Monroe, Vincent van Gogh, Thomas Chatterton, and Socrates.

The San Francisco Golden Gate Bridge has been the jumping-off place for many suicides. The first was Harold Wobber, on August 8, 1937, just seventy-three days after it opened. He died an instant death after hitting the water 238 feet below.[2] Few survive that leap, but one whose attempt failed stated six years later, "People become depressed because they have desires and they are not fulfilled. If a person could just realize that those desires are not going to be answered by *wanting* them."[3]

Desire and expectation are potent drives—the very stuff of which life, with all its shades of meaning, is comprised. Why is it that some are driven to suicidal despair and others with

93

unmet desires and expectations manage to survive without giving in? Certainly the hopeful balance of expectation and reality keeps most from despair, along with the recognition that these drives must be reckoned with.

Suicide among Minorities

People from all races, creeds, and cultural backgrounds kill themselves. Southern blacks living in rural areas seldom take their lives, but the statistics change drastically in the northern part of the United States. In New York City the suicide rate for blacks regularly exceeds the rate for whites. Among research psychiatrists and sociologists whose careers have touched the lives of suicidal black people, there is general agreement that anger plays a leading role in suicide, especially among black women. One psychiatrist at a Harlem hospital explained that in observing younger men and women, he saw great disappointments that were experienced very early in life. Those disappointments led to an overwhelming sense of rage and frustration, which ultimately led to suicide attempts when the rage and frustration became combined with the sense that nothing was going to change. Poverty and crime play into the disturbing forces that propel a person into a suicidal mood. Many suicidal people come from multiproblem or dysfunctional families.

When minorities move from rural to urban areas, and from south to north, there is often a resulting breakdown of families, unemployment or job instability, cramped tenements, and other factors that contribute to rage and frustration. Among blacks, Hispanics, and American Indians, the suicide rate drops after age forty-four. This is interesting in contrast with the pattern among whites, where the risk of suicide rises with increasing age.[4]

The Urban Indian and the Reservation Indian

Studies of the Indian population in this country have un-covered a virtual suicide epidemic among males between fif-teen and twenty-four years of age, accounting for 64 percent of all suicides by Native Americans (this includes American Indians and Alaska Natives).[5] The problems they face relate to identity—caught between two cultures, neither an Indian with a sense of pride and respect for their people and their culture nor an assimilated outsider able to identify with the culture and traditions of the dominant group. The result is psychological chaos.

An Indian counselor at a Denver treatment center for In-dian alcoholics, in speaking of the high incidence of suicide among Indians, said, "They have two choices, either drink-ing or suicide. When you have no hope, you contemplate drinking or suicide." He pointed out that they are haunted by alcoholism, unemployment, and suicide, whether on the reservation or in the city. In reflecting on the suicide of Chris, a twenty-year-old Indian with a chronic mental health prob-lem who turned to panhandling to support himself and lived in bushes and vacant houses, this counselor listed the causes of suicide among Indians as "low self-esteem, no family dy-namics, no firm sense of who they are and complete loss of cultural values."

I read the story of Chris, whose hopelessness caught up with him. He fashioned a rope out of a blue towel, tied one end to bars in his Denver County Jail cell, and slipped the noose at the other end around his neck. The jailers, doctors who were called in to care for the street people, and his pan-handler buddies called him "quiet and gentle, a very likeable guy," a young man who never started fights, who liked to joke around. The shock waves that flooded over his street friends found them turning to a young Baptist minister who ran a coffee-house ministry on the street nearby where so many of these young men hung out. "I didn't think I had made any inroads [with these hard-core alcoholic drifters] until Chris died. But the Indians came here to the church to grieve. They cried and wept. . . . It moved me," the pastor said.

A psychiatrist at the county jail pointed to the suicide victim's court records, which showed he had been in jail forty-four times in the thirty-six months before he died. "He had that sad appearance which was always typical of him. He was a committed street person with an alcoholism problem. He really exemplified the chronically mentally ill. It is the highlight of their week when they get arrested. Jail is the best thing they've got. It is so sad. So sad. He had been to jail so many times."[6]

Status Integration, Geographic Mobility

Sometimes when things get better for someone, they can also get worse. An anomaly. Where there was low aspiration, an individual can sink into an acceptance of the status quo. If, however, things start improving, the person becomes more aware and then starts worrying about reaching expected economic and social potential. When this potential is not reached or the momentum is too slow, it can be devastating. A move from poverty to middle class has, in some cases, precipitated an increase in suicide. Keeping up with the Joneses becomes a rat race. Sensing that others are looking down their noses at you because you haven't yet quite arrived can be demeaning. Mean-spiritedness is only too real. Intolerance exists.

Because we are an increasingly mobile society, it can be very disheartening to attempt to be friendly and integrate oneself and one's family into new surroundings only to be regarded with suspicion and have one's efforts rebuffed. Those of us who have lived in various places can tell you it's real. This can be extremely difficult for children and teenagers, and parents need to be sensitive to their feelings.

Opening Our Eyes to the Light

In the book of Ecclesiastes, we are told that there is a time to be born and a time to die (see Eccles. 3:2). How much better to let God decide when and how we die. But we are not prepared for death until we have learned how to live.

Dorothy Sayers pointed to Christ's earthly walk as "passing through the world like a flame." Is it any wonder the Gospel writer portrays him as "true Light, which lighteth every man" (John 1:9 KJV)? It is characteristic of light to shine forth. Light is self-evidencing. It makes itself known. God is the original of life and light, and the manifestation of himself through Jesus was evidence of the Father's desire to impart that eternal life into those who will believe in and accept this glorious light. How much we need to be flames that stay lit! How sad when flameout occurs at one's own hand!

Shine through me, Father, shine through me. May that be our prayer as we seek to help others come to the light that can dispel their darkness. By any name, by any method, suicide is a senseless tragedy.

❦ 9 ❦

Sad, Young, and Wanting to Die

I wish I could tell Mother how torn I am—like two people pulling me apart. The Good One and the Bad One, and I'm going to die in the middle.

An unidentified child who failed in a suicide attempt

They swallow poison.
Dart into heavy traffic.
Slash their wrists.
Beat and disfigure themselves.
Overdose on medicine and drugs.
Hang themselves.

In
these
and
other
grim
ways
they self-destruct—the child suicides.

I was eleven years old. Life was just so pathetically empty. I remember taking a bottle of medicine I found in the medicine cabinet. I knew it was poisonous because it had a skull and crossbones on it. When no one was looking, I mixed it with peanut butter and spread it on a piece of bread. Then I ate it, went upstairs, and crawled in bed.

"Later I awoke and was disappointed that I wasn't dead. I really didn't even feel very sick. (I guess I didn't get enough from one piece of bread.) Still later I was glad I hadn't died. I couldn't understand myself—one day wanting to be dead, the next day glad to be alive even though our circumstances hadn't changed. I wondered then if life was always going to be that way.

"My parents were terribly religious in a frightening sort of way—always talking about God coming to destroy the world and taking the good people away first. I didn't think a God who did that could be very nice. For a long time I spent endless hours trying to figure out how to dig a big tunnel I could run to and escape from that kind of a God when he came. I finally gave up on that project.

"I gave up on God about then too.

"But I didn't give up on the idea of killing myself. I always held it out to myself as a last resort. Sort of a 'Well, kid, you know you can always kill yourself when things get too bad.'"

I sat there listening to the hairdresser, having taken time out on a trip to have some work done on my hair. She had a small black booklet lying on the counter. In bright red letters I read, SUICIDE. When I questioned her about the book and her interest in the subject of suicide, she shared with me her unhappiness as a child, the sadness that pervaded her being as she moved into her teens, and the four attempts to take her life. Each, obviously, had failed.

An Eclipse of the Soul

"How old are you now?" I asked.

Shamefully she glanced down, then looked at me in the mirror. "I'm only twenty-three," she replied.

And so we talked. We talked of suicide and being sad, young, and wanting to die. God certainly makes no mistakes. My sitting there in her chair was an appointment with destiny for sure. I silently thanked God for having me cancel a previous appointment and, on an impulse, checking in at this hotel shop instead.

As we talked I learned that it was the assistance she received at a Teen Challenge Center that finally checked her suicide impulses and helped her get her life straightened out. Still, she had some questions and needed someone with whom she could talk. Providentially, she had no more appointments that afternoon, and I was free also. We talked and talked.

"I know I'll never try suicide again," she said. "I've gotten answers to my questions in surprising ways—like today." And she smiled.

I couldn't help wondering how many there are like her—children giving up on life when they are so very young, teenagers struggling with the complexities of growing up, and young people uneasy about their future.

The Divorce Factor; Troubled Family Situations

For many young people, their world has collapsed around them. With 50 percent of the marriages in the country ending in divorce, a large proportion of children and young people live in one-parent households. But the breakup of the home is not the only contributing factor. Many single-parent homes fare very well, with children, adolescents, or teenagers who are well-adjusted, bright, and happy. Sometimes the stress within a home where the marriage partners are in an almost constant state of anger with each other and where bitter words are tossed about causes the children to be fearful, angry themselves, and experiencing a host of emotions they are unprepared to handle. The result is frightened, insecure, and upset children.

A family crisis can precipitate suicide attempts. About 71 percent of young people who attempt suicide are from broken homes. Close to 75 percent of teens from broken homes reported that they felt guilty and responsible for the divorce. Divorce can stimulate a suicide attempt because a child may feel that if he or she is out of the way, things just might work out. Of the 29 percent of suicide attempters who come from unbroken homes, many are living in very troubled family situations.[1]

Many parents are too busy and preoccupied with their own lives to pay attention to their children, particularly when the children become teenagers. The Columbine killings and the suicides of the two young men who were responsible found many of us gasping in disbelief: How could the parents not know? Didn't they ever check their sons' bedrooms? Didn't they know what their sons were up to?

We react similarly to other school killings. I have files full of stories of these terrible events. We've all seen the headlines and watched the television coverage. Here are some of the contributing factors to troubled youth and youth suicide:

Parents make little or no effort to try to comprehend what their children are saying and thinking. This lack of communication between parents and children is a frightening reality. One statistic reveals that 88 percent of youth suicides occurred at home, very often with parents in the next room. The most important thing parents can do is to listen—really listen hard—to what their children are trying to communicate.

Ineffectual father-son or mother-daughter relationships put the suicidal young person under great pressure to live up to parental expectations. It is not unusual for loving, well-meaning parents to encourage a child to make something of himself or herself. But sometimes parents push too hard for self-serving reasons. One public-health professional points out that some parents need their children to achieve to make up for their own feelings of inadequacy. Healthy self-esteem is more than pride. It has to do with feelings of adequacy to cope with daily life. Feeling good about oneself can be nurtured in a child, but it should not be forced upon the youngster with the idea that he or she had better succeed and not make the parent ashamed.

Parents substitute their authority for honest answers to their children's questions. "Just because I say so" is no answer to a young person's request for reasons why he or she should or should not do something. Young people deserve our understanding and respect. This may call for extra patience on the part of parents, and this takes time. Some children commit suicide as a protest against the perceived, if not real, legalism of parental authority.

Parents set bad examples for their children with their own use of drugs and alcohol. Substance abuse is a major problem among suicidal young people. The use of such substances should always be regarded as a cry for help. Drug and alcohol abuse is often a symptom of a deeper problem and not the cause of the trouble. Substance abuse is a self-destructive trait, and parents need to take control and get their children help.

Parents do not know their children's friends. Every child should have the benefit of growing up firmly grounded in the book of Proverbs. *The Living Bible* version is just tremendous in putting into today's vernacular exactly what impressionable young minds need to hear. Proverbs 1:10 reads like this: "If young toughs tell you, 'Come and join us'—turn your back on them!" This quote from *The Living Bible* is an illustration of the importance of choosing one's friends carefully.

Parents fail in providing the right set of values. Many children grow up having too much; they have not been trained to accept responsibility, nor do they appreciate the work ethic. Easy come, easy go. With their values askew, they play with their toys—their expensive cars, boats, stereos, and electronic equipment—with little or no concept of what the worth is. They dress in the latest styles, mimicking their favorite musicians and stars. Belly buttons exposed on girls in their tight-fitting tank tops and sweaters, and other faddish ways of dressing are suggestive and can be seductive. Their attire itself can get them into trouble. They may be surrounded by affluence but feel deprived, not in material possessions but in emotional support. When none of their possessions brings the ultimate in satisfaction, they become disillusioned. A form of suicide contagion can set in, which helps explain why many times you will hear about multiple suicides among young people in a given locale.

Movies, television, and song lyrics glamorize promiscuous sex, death, and other morbid practices. Parents who have allowed unsupervised watching and listening will have children, adolescents, and young people whose impressions and values are totally out of sync with normalcy. The influence of these skewed values is to make young people romanticize both the nature of death and the effect it would have on the people around them.

Parents have not established religious moorings nor helped their children understand the need for a relationship with their Creator and the development of a faith that sustains them in times of trouble. The family that applies the Bible's teachings and consistently and appropriately holds up such values and teachings as the standard for wise and happy living will assuredly stand the despondent young person in good stead. Young people need to be a part of youth activities and church life. To fail in providing this is to open the door to other influences that may precipitate suicidal feelings when the stresses of home, school, and relationships tumble in. Children need a strong anchor. The church can help provide this. Children and young people from Christian homes do attempt suicide also, and some of them succeed. The church that holds out help, hope, love, and nonjudgmental attitudes and provides opportunities for discussion and doesn't set up barriers to open communication goes a long way to thwart suicide attempts. Kids are living with a lot of emotional pain; they need someone to talk to whom they trust. Adults in the church who show interest in what's going on in the lives of these young people and make themselves available, showing them they understand and truly care, will find young people responding to the love of Jesus they see in you.

Family trust is missing. Troubled adolescents rebel against suspicious parents, yet parents have the responsibility and the right to know about their children's friends and behavior. Parents who fail to discuss the facts of life and provide sex education in the home leave the door open for possible experimentation with resultant tragic consequences. This experimentation may even propel young people, daughters in particular, to a suicide attempt.

Parents fail to discipline their children. Enforcement of curfews and family rules is essential. Taking away privileges is a proper way to reinforce such disciplinary measures. Temper tantrums in small children need to be dealt with appropriately. Rage and violence must be brought under control, or parents will reap the harvest of failure to do so in their children's later years. Failure to discipline can be interpreted as a lack of caring. Children need the assurance that they are loved.

Parents are not home when children need them. This is complicated by the fact that in so many homes both parents work. Unsupervised children can get into trouble. Unsupervised children can form bad habits. Less available parenting has left children and adolescents with little emotional backup.

Responsibility for suicidal behavior or completed suicide cannot be ascribed solely to dysfunctional families or just to family dynamics themselves. More than one professional emphasizes that this is not only unfair but unwise. However, if someone identifies with the material presented here, he or she can take a giant step in the right direction to make changes, and the lives of family members might be spared. To shore up and improve the crumbling structure of the American family is always in order.

Accident Prone or Suicide Bent?

Children who repeatedly injure themselves may not simply be accident prone but may be suicidal, according to a study published in the *American Journal of Psychiatry.* If the injured child's history indicates that he or she is living in a highly stressful environment involving abuse or neglect, such a child needs careful monitoring. Abnormal aggression in a child might be suggestive of latent problems. Teachers and care providers are in the best position to make such determinations. Psychiatrists recommend questioning children about their accidents, noting that "children will readily admit suicidal intent if it is present."[2]

Many suicides go unreported, and often so-called accidental injuries and poisonings in school-age children are purposeful, self-destructive acts, or they may signal abuse and neglect.

Emotional Poverty

Here are stories from my files that are illustrative of the emotional poverty of some children that led to suicide attempts.

A six-year-old boy wanted to die—"Because nobody loves me," he said. He first cut himself with his father's razor before being rescued from a second-story window where he tried to hang himself.

A twelve-year-old girl survived an overdose of pills found in the medicine cabinet at her home. "I would be better off dead," she explained. "Then no one would ever have to look at my ugly face again." She had hung her doll by its neck, tried to drug her little sister, cut both her legs with scissors, and slashed her wrists before overdosing.

"Mother doesn't have any love for me," cried an eleven-year-old boy who tried to kill his dog, attempted to suffocate his baby brother with a pillow, and stabbed pins into his stomach.

When children witness family violence, both verbal and physical, it can precipitate acute panic, fear, and concern that they may be the next victim of a violent assault.

Such children are considered at risk for suicide by health providers. Their actions sound more like something out of a horror movie than real life. But there are children whose actions reveal the symptoms of emotional poverty. Many of them have a preoccupation with self-destruction.

Hospitals and emergency shelters see battered and abused children who, in sheer desperation and panic, try to take their own lives. Not all are as philosophical as one ten-year-old whose thirteen-year-old brother had committed suicide earlier. He said, "Everyone kills and everyone dies. There is no escape," in hopeless resignation to his own sad fate.

Suicide Clusters

News stories in recent years have reported clusters of suicides in a school or locale, among ordinary youngsters (teenagers especially) with no easily apparent problems. (This is also mentioned briefly in chapter 5.) So the obvious question understandably becomes "Why?" Why, according to the American Association of Suicidology statistics, does an average of one young person under the age of twenty-five commit suicide every two hours and eleven minutes? Suicide remains the third leading cause of death among the younger population.

Two counselors at two high schools in southern California have said that the subject they have to address most often with students who come in for counseling is the subject of suicide. It is a subject that weighs heavily on their minds and on which they contemplate. Young people are not immune from feeling a concern about the nation and the world.

They have high aspirations, dreams, and hopes but live in a society that is becoming increasingly complex. Childhood and young adult depression is very common but too often is not acknowledged nor given attention by the child's parents or caregivers.

You may remember these news stories:

In a twelve-month period, seven teenagers in Plano, Texas, committed suicide, four by carbon-monoxide poisoning, three by guns.

Five boys in New York's Westchester and Putnam counties died by their own hand, four of them by hanging.

In Houston, Texas, the suicides of six high school students in a two-month period jolted the community.

One student at a high school in Spencer, Massachusetts, killed himself, and at least two schoolmates, possibly four, tried to extinguish their own lives and failed.

A spree of self-destruction in an Omaha, Nebraska, high school sent a shock wave through the school, which became branded "Suicide High." Hysteria swept over the part of town where the tragedies occurred as three students committed suicide within five days. Four others tried but failed.

In Spanaway, Washington, a failed romance and bad grades caused a fourteen-year-old girl to fatally shoot her ex-boyfriend and another boy at their junior high school before killing herself.

Eight teenagers on an Indian reservation in Wyoming committed suicide one after another.

A high school in Helena, Montana, had eighteen cases of suicide in one year.

Two young people playing at being grown-up too early in life, a Romeo and Juliet dream, ended their lives in Scotts Valley, California, when they taped a garden hose to the exhaust of the young man's brand-new Ford pickup, turned on the ignition, and waited to die.

Sadly, we hear stories and statistics about youth suicides far too often. What can be done? How does one stop suicidal contemplation?

Suicide Prevention and Intervention

First, here are some telltale signs that children, adolescents, or young people may be suicidal. (These signs are not very different from those mentioned in chapter 5 but are given here in more detail.)

- *A change in mood.* They tend to cry or be sad, to get little pleasure from anything, and to want to be alone.
- *Noticeable changes in eating or sleeping patterns.* Depressed adolescents may overeat or eat unusually little; they may sleep more than usual, not at all, or only at odd times.
- *Adolescents may see themselves differently.* They may talk about feeling ugly or worthless and put themselves down.
- *Difficulty in concentrating.* They may be more agitated or more lethargic, doing nothing but listening to music or watching TV. Where they have been good students, now their grades tumble.

Some parents would argue that such behavior isn't unusual among adolescents in particular. It is true that normal-thinking young people go through personality changes, but they shouldn't become moody or sullen, do poorly in school, or want to listen to their stereos all day. The point is to watch out for excessive behaviors.

Two other things may show a young person becoming preoccupied with thoughts of suicide.

1. **Communication.** In eight out of ten cases, suicidal adolescents will communicate their intent to someone, if not their parents. So all suicidal gesturing and statements such as "Do you have to be crazy to shoot yourself?" or "I'm going to heaven very soon," or some such unusual comment should be taken seriously. Take veiled threats about dying very seriously. Some remarks may not be so veiled, and you might wrongly assume the young person is making a joke. Any indication of a preoccupation with death should be looked into. A preoccupation with putting things in order and giving away prized possessions could be a tip-off that something is wrong.

2. **Depression.** Kids need to be taught that depression is common, that it's okay to feel mad, sad, or upset. They must be helped to see and understand that if they will just be patient, they will feel better. If the depression doesn't seem to lift, then seek professional help. Explain that it is not uncommon for people to need to be on some kind of medication, that in all likelihood it may not have to be of long duration. Don't cave in if the child wants to stop seeing a professional, and supervise the taking of medicine. Some depressed individuals will tongue the pill (put it under their tongues and spit it out when the parent or caregiver isn't around).

Sometimes the cause of teenagers' depression is not easily identified. But there are some things to be aware of.

Loss. Has there been a recent loss—for instance, of a parent through death or divorce, or of some other relative or friend? One young child's grandmother passed away, and she had been his caregiver. His depression was obvious, acute, and of long duration. He required help. Dr. Archibald Hart points out that the general conclusion among researchers is that while divorce doesn't condemn a child to years of depression, it does make a child more depression prone. Hart also points out that the most common cause of male depression is the effect of divorce and parental turmoil on boys, and the evidence is quite clear on this point.[3]

Broken relationships. Has there been a breakup with a girl-friend or boyfriend? An enormous number of teenage suicides can be traced to just such a broken relationship.

Disappointment. Has the teenager suffered a disappointment in failing to make it on the soccer team or some other such sport or activity that meant a lot more to him or her than anyone realized? Teenagers' egos are fragile. Don't ignore something like this.

Cynicism. Cynicism and pessimism among kids is widespread these days. They've been sold the idea that college is going to pave the road to happiness, but some of them aren't going to make it to the likes of a Harvard or Stanford. They may have to settle for a couple years of community college and work to put some money aside and seek grants or scholarships. There is nothing wrong with that except that some of their peers may disparage it. That is not going to make them feel very good. They need to be challenged to see that their hopes for the future can be realized but that it isn't going to happen overnight. They need lots of encouragement, reassurance, and strong moral support.

Loneliness. Lots of teenagers are lonely. They may put on a good front and to all appearances succeed at bluffing their way along, but underneath is that hole of emptiness. Perhaps seeing all this in print has made you more aware of the need to be there for your children—available so they can talk and so you can talk. "Don't give up. Don't even think about suicide or copping out, because I can get you away from the pain without you dying." You think that's pretty extreme talk? Well, think again. Many troubled, lonely, discouraged, depressed individuals—especially teenagers—see death as an attractive alternative to the accumulative stresses they are subjected to. For some, suicide becomes a way to find peace and escape, while for others, it is a statement of protest and rage. Teenagers are too young to realize that this too shall pass.

Some Alarming Statistical Facts

According to latest available statistical information, here are additional facts about youth suicide that present a picture that is quite alarming:

Whereas suicides accounted for 1.3 percent of all deaths in the U.S. annually, they comprised 12.7 percent of all deaths among fifteen- to twenty-four-year-olds. Each year, there are approximately ten youth suicides for every one hundred thousand youth.

In the past sixty years, the suicide rate has quadrupled for males fifteen to twenty-four years old and has doubled for females of the same age.

Firearms remain the most commonly used suicide method among youth, accounting for 52 percent of all completed suicides. Research shows that the access to and the availability of firearms is a significant factor in observed increases in rates of youth suicide. Guns in the home are deadly to its occupants!

Suicide by suffocation among ten- to fourteen-year-olds has occurred more frequently than those by firearms since 1999.

For every completed suicide by youth, it is estimated that one hundred to two hundred attempts are made. A prior suicide attempt is an important risk factor for an eventual completion. Most adolescent suicides occur after school hours and in the teen's home. Although rates vary somewhat by geographic location, within a typical high school classroom, it is likely that three students (one boy and two girls) have made a suicide attempt in the past year. The typical profile of an adolescent nonfatal suicide attempter is a female who ingests pills, while the profile of the typical completer suicide is a male who dies from a gunshot wound.

In 2002, 260 children ages ten to fourteen completed suicide in the U.S.[4]

Some Dos and Don'ts for Helping a Troubled Teen

- Do trust your instincts if you suspect your teenager is suicidal.
- Do communicate your concern. Listen to his or her problems. Show your support. Suicidal kids just want to know that someone cares.
- Do seek professional help from a school counselor, minister, or psychologist. Just make sure that the professional is listening to God. If you are uncertain where to get help, look on the Internet or turn to the Yellow Pages. (See also appendix A.) There is a profusion of material available. The U.S. Public Health Service, the National Institute of Mental Health, local suicide prevention centers, libraries, and bookstores will provide material for anyone who wishes to pursue the study of suicidal behavior in more detail.
- Do remove items such as guns, potentially lethal medications, and alcohol from your home.
- Don't leave your teenager alone if you have any suspicion at all that suicide is imminent.
- Don't act shocked at what a teenager might tell you.

- Don't debate with your teenager about whether suicide is wrong or right. It may make him or her feel more guilty and intensify the depression.

Finally, remember that the root of all suicides is a sense of hopelessness, a feeling that things will not get better. For troubled young people, the lack of life experiences to draw upon leaves them very vulnerable and puts a crisis in a most desperate perspective. Troubled teens need to hear a message of hope and support from people who love them. Walk with them through their pain. Turn to the beginning of this book and read some of those verses from the book of Psalms (pages 17–21) that saw me through the crisis in my soul; point them out to those who are hurting and troubled.

✿10✿

Depression and Suicide among the Older Population

Grow old along with me!
The best is yet to be,
The last of life, for which the first was made.

Robert Browning

Annually, older people top the list of completed suicides. The American Association of Suicidology reports that an average of one older person kills himself or herself every ninety-five minutes. For these members of the older generation, the immortal words of Robert Browning have no meaning.

Before writing this chapter, I reread Sherwood Eliot Wirt's book *I Don't Know What Old Is, but Old Is Older than Me.* What an upbeat, optimistic book full of the wit and humor that have always characterized Dr. Wirt's life! You can't help but catch his refreshing and spirited outlook when you read such things as "For me life is an ice cream social. . . . I take issue with the conventional view of old people. I refuse to be dumped!"[1] Dr. Wirt was already more than eighty years old when he wrote the book. He contended that life in one's senior years need not be uninteresting or without vital significance and meaning. How much that joy-filled note needs to be sounded!

I Don't Know What Old Is, but Old Is Older than Me is a reflection of what characterized Dr. Wirt's entire life, but it is also a recognition on his part that the number-one problem among older people is not aging itself but a lack of vision, and he wasn't talking about cataracts! This vision is what one thinks of life on earth and how one fits in. And that doesn't have to diminish with advancing age. Dr. Wirt puts it like this:

> Put me in a rocking chair without a vision, and I would languish. Put me in a room full of people sitting in rocking chairs with nothing to do, and I would not last long. If I had to stay there, I would certainly organize something—perhaps a game of "Pictionary" or even a prayer meeting. But give me a vision of something new and challenging God would have me do, something that would fire my spirit, get the elan flowing, and give me an opportunity to use my life to help others, and I will feel as young as I do now, and as I did at forty, the difference being that today I am a lot smarter![2]

Whether called a "senior citizen," "one of the old folks," or "chronologically gifted," those of us sixty-five and over, here we are, some in top-notch shape, hale and hearty. Others . . . well, there are some aches and pains, there have been some quite serious health problems, we've been through wars and recessions, we've held down jobs, we've raised our kids, we've helped them acquire an education, and we've looked forward to retirement. All of us lost loved ones along the way—grandparents, parents, mates, aunts, uncles, brothers, sisters, maybe even some children or friends. But the life cycle continues—and now we may find ourselves not only with an empty nest, the children having flown away and established their own nests, but also widows or widowers. I can remember the time when I looked up to and respected my elders; now I am the elder. I love the way Dr. Wirt puts it: "We are not 'old folks' any more; we are simply folks who are older."[3] Well put! What I feel is wiser.

So why are the forgotten elderly bowing out by suicidal means? Having financial independence makes the transition into older age much more enjoyable. Many don't have that. Also, having one's mental faculties still intact is a distinct plus. When one's health deteriorates, advancing age and its accompanying challenges can make getting older very difficult. The senior years can also be a time when one has to make the adjustment to solitude, when one's life partner is no longer living. The suffering occasioned by loss of one's spouse is made worse by this feeling of solitude. The loneliness that gnaws at the heart of so many older people is real. Others learn to deal with their loneliness in some creative ways—pursuing hobbies, taking up something new, taking advantage of more time for leisure activities, traveling, reading.

For years I've been thinking about writing a book entitled *A Funny Thing Happened on My Way to Retirement*, but much of what I've uncovered from others hasn't been so funny. Retirement for some turns into nonexistence, with the rocking chair claiming another victim. Some people feel that life is passing them by. They either have short memories or choose not to enjoy the good memories—not that one should live in the past, but to think that there's not much more to life just because one isn't a part of the day-to-day action of the working world shrieks of something gone wrong in one's thinking. So we aren't in the middle of all that's going on—does that mean there is no longer any meaning to existence? This may be the erroneous thinking that propels some older adults into suicide. It also reveals a poverty in one's capacity to look around and see where one could help others, what one could do to take advantage of some activities designed with seniors in mind, how one could use one's talents, the unique God-given gifts and resources one has. We have so much to give from our wealth of experience. We could be mentoring some younger person, even offering our services by reading in a school or library program, any number of things if one applied oneself to thinking through different options. Remember, it's what Dr. Wirt calls the number-one problem with older people—a lack of vision. All of which points to the importance of looking at the "Why?" behind senior suicide. Why is the suicide rate highest for white men eighty-five and older: thirty-five suicides per one hundred thousand, about 4.6 times the current rate for all ages of eleven per one hundred thousand? Older Americans are disproportionately likely to commit suicide, so why, while they make up 12.3 percent of the population, do they account for almost 17.5 percent of all suicides? What this shows is that in 2002, there were about fifteen elderly suicides each day, resulting in 5,548 suicides among those sixty-five and older.[4]

Problems That Contribute to a Desire to End It All

Certainly it is true that health problems create situations in which the elderly long for relief. Some of the biggies include cancer, strokes, heart disease, arteriosclerosis, and other degenerative diseases and debilitating factors. There may come a time when elderly people are confined to wheelchairs and can no longer take care of all their own needs. Failing eyesight, joint replacements, diabetes, loss of hearing. Many are the health concerns that might make it necessary for the elderly to have live-in help, or be placed in a nursing-care facility, or live with their children. This is very hard. To be forced to give up one's home, in addition to facing the health crisis itself, creates the kind of unthinkable scenarios we always hoped we'd never have to face. A permanent out seems better than four walls, little or no companionship, and the suffering that can accompany ill health.

It was interesting to me to find that 85 percent of elderly suicides were male and that the number of male suicides in late life was five and a half times greater than for female suicides. The rate of suicide for women declines after age sixty (after peaking in middle adulthood, ages forty-five to forty-nine). White men over the age of eighty-five, are considered the "old-old," and they are at the greatest risk of all age-gender-race groups.[5]

Family caregivers need to understand this, and Dr. Paul Tournier's assessment in *Learn to Grow Old* can help put this mind-set into a good framework. He writes,

> It is a great trial to become entirely dependent upon someone else, and it is in the great trials that one can measure people's spiritual resources. . . . Nevertheless, the loss of one's independence is always a great trial. Before it happens, all old people fear it. It is for that reason that so many old people stubbornly refuse to be transferred to an old people's home. . . . It is frightening! . . . Cut off from their past, their environment . . . they become depersonalized, and are no more than numbers. This is the triumph of an impersonalized society. . . . They have already suffered a serious shock merely by being uprooted: The change is one of the worst traumas that the old person has to undergo.[6]

119

It should be noted that although older adults *attempt* suicide less often than those in other age groups, they have a higher completion rate. For all ages combined, there is an estimated one suicide for every twenty-five attempts. Over the age of sixty-five, there is one estimated suicide for every four attempts. Firearms are the most common means (72 percent) used for completing suicide among the elderly. Men (79 percent) use firearms more than twice as often as women (33 percent). Alcohol or substance abuse plays a diminishing role in later-life suicides compared to younger suicides.[7]

One of my friends goes once a week to a retirement home, where she reads to the residents. The reasons for them being there are, for the most part, not visible to her, but she has become acquainted with some of the residents and their situations. Oftentimes she finds herself wondering why some of them are even there. Where are their families? When we speak of the forgotten elderly, it is such as these who come to mind. Many never receive visits from family members or friends. My friend regards these dear people, especially the lovely ladies, as parent or grandparent figures. She told of one sweet woman who provided fifty thousand dollars for her granddaughter to adopt two children, yet this granddaughter has never brought the children (the oldest being six) to visit their great-grandmother. Can you imagine it? Out of the largesse of her beautiful heart, this woman has done this for her granddaughter, who cannot have children of her own. Yet the granddaughter is so lacking in love, respect, and gratitude that she hasn't come to see her grandmother with these children in six years! Think of the heartbreak of the grandmother! The disappointment. The aching longing. That is the kind of circumstance that could very easily find a senior citizen longing for release from the pain of living. How insensitive and selfish this grandchild is!

Tournier pointed out that using home health-care services or live-in help is much to be preferred rather than institutionalizing an older family member. When this can no longer be done, then of course, hospitalization or moving one's loved one to a retirement center is the answer.

Some years ago it was my joy to get to know Gladys Lindberg, a pioneer in the field of nutrition, whose incredible insights and loving concern and counsel helped thousands, including myself, get on the path to robust health. Then it became my privilege to help Gladys and her daughter, Judy Lindberg McFarland, write the book *Take Charge of Your Health*. Gladys lived well into her eighties, always the picture of radiant health.

In more recent years, her daughter, Judy, wrote the book *Aging without Growing Old*. Without question, the body needs sufficient and balanced quantities of nutrients in order to achieve optimal health. It has been conclusively shown that nutritional deficiencies are the precursor of declining health. In her book Judy combines her mother's timeless wisdom with cutting-edge research and provides information showing how the way we live and what we eat may dramatically alter the aging process. I am convinced that those longing for optimal health regardless of their age need this information.

For those who have given up on life and who have succumbed to depression, my recommendation is that you obtain Judy's book and take charge of your health. The general principles she writes about regarding health and good nutrition have stood the test of time. You have nothing to lose and everything to gain.

Late-Life Depression

One of the leading causes of suicide among the elderly is depression, often undiagnosed or untreated. The National Institute of Mental Health and the Centers for Disease Control report that as many as three out of every one hundred people over age sixty-five suffer from clinical depression and that the suicide rate is twice as high in this population compared to other age groups.

In contrast to the normal emotional experiences of sadness, grief, loss, or passing mood states, depressive disorders can be extreme and persistent and can interfere significantly with an individual's ability to function.

Clinical depression is an illness, a chemical imbalance in the brain, and it can strike people regardless of age, race, or economic position. In contrast to the normal emotional experiences of sadness, grief, loss, or passing mood states, depressive disorders can be extreme and persistent and can interfere significantly with an individual's ability to function.

Depression itself, however, should not be considered a normal part of aging. When it does occur, often it accompanies other medical illnesses such as cardiovascular disease, stroke, diabetes, and cancer. Such health problems, as well as various social and economic difficulties, conspire to cause late-life depression and suicidal symptoms to go underdiagnosed and undertreated.

Research and various treatment options are available, and if a loved one or you yourself are experiencing depression symptoms, it is my hope and prayer that you will find someone who understands and can prescribe a course of treatment.

While doing this chapter, I took down a favorite book from my library written by "oldtimer" revivalist Vance Havner. His humor and great attitude played a role in his longevity as he passed the biblical landmark of "threescore years and ten" (Ps.

90:10). In reminiscing about men he had worked with through the years who were no longer living, he said he felt like he was "the last leaf left on the tree," and that "anything after seventy is a postscript and a bonus." He quoted "The world passeth away, and the lust thereof; but he that doeth the will of God abideth forever" (1 John 2:17 KJV), calling this "an ageless theme that the years cannot dim nor time outdate." You would have to agree that this kind of thinking would keep depression away! As dear Vance Havner would say, "If a person sets out to do God's will he has known life's greatest adventure."[8]

Demoralizing Attitudes

Speaking of attitudes, Dr. Charles Swindoll, in *Strengthening Your Grip*, writes about four attitudes among older individuals that come from our humanity, not from the Lord. These attitudes are, therefore, very demoralizing. They include *uselessness*, the feeling that causes people to say, "I'm over the hill," or "I just get in your way," or "I don't have much to contribute anymore, so I'll just back off from life." Swindoll points out that it is not uncommon to find that those who once played an extremely significant role in life feel the most useless as the sands of time cover their past achievements.

Another attitude is that of *guilt*. "[It is] an awful companion. . . . And yet guilt has a way of hijacking our minds as age slows our steps and sensitizes our memories. . . . With more time on our hands, we yield to guilt's finger of blame and to the frowns of 'Shame on you!' Inevitably, feelings of dissatisfaction growl and churn within . . . [and they can] slam us to the mat. Guilt is a coward and bully, forever picking fights we can't seem to win," says Swindoll.[9]

Then there is *self-pity*, the "woe is me" syndrome. Self-pity uses a lot of blame and bitterness in its vocabulary.

Fear, Swindoll believes, is the most common attitude among those who are getting on in years—economic fears, fear of losing one's health or mind, fear of losing one's mate or friends. "To strengthen our grip on aging, these feelings must somehow be counteracted."[10]

Suicide Pacts

A northern California newspaper carried the distressing news that an elderly man shot and killed his wife in their home and then, turning the .45-caliber automatic on himself, committed suicide. The couple left a note citing failing health as the reason. Such accounts are not uncommon among the elderly.

I read an account in *Time* magazine about the suicide pact carried out by a seventy-seven-year-old retired preeminent New Jersey pastor and his eighty-year-old wife. They took overdoses of sleeping pills in their Princeton home. It was reported that she died quickly but he vomited up the pills and was found and taken to a hospital, where he died a month later of a heart attack. He was a nonstop churchman, heading New York's Union Theological Seminary at its pinnacle of influence. But when he suffered a stroke, he was forced into retirement. The stroke left him with speech that was largely incomprehensible. That, of course, was a terrible frustration for a man with his verbal skill. His wife suffered from arthritis and had undergone two hip replacement surgeries. But their suicide pact was not made under the extreme conditions of terminal illness that often prompts such pacts. They wrote a note that said, "We are both increasingly weak and unwell, and who would want to die in a nursing home?"[11]

There was divergence of opinion among the theologian's friends, whom *Time* magazine called "A *Who's Who* of liberal

Protestantism." But the magazine reported that his colleagues were, for the most part, sympathetic. His suicide note declared that theirs was a responsible decision that "will become more usual and acceptable as the years pass."

The Traditional Judeo-Christian View

Dietrich Bonhoeffer held a different view from the Union Theological Seminary theologian. (Bonhoeffer, interestingly, was an illustrious Union Theological Seminary alumnus himself.) This German pastor and theologian could have stayed in the United States, but when the Nazis under Hitler came to power, he went back to Germany and directed an underground seminary for the Lutheran church. For his participation in the plot against Hitler, he was, by the personal order of Heinrich Himmler, hanged at Flossenburg concentration camp a month before the end of the war in Europe.

Bonhoeffer's notable books are among the most important writings of the twentieth century. He stood in opposition to suicide and stated, "God has reserved to Himself the right to determine the end of life, because He alone knows the goal to which it is His will to lead it. Even if [a person's] earthly life has become a torment for him, he must commit it intact to God's hands, from which it came." Bonhoeffer expressed what has always been one of the bedrock tenets of Judeo-Christendom.

The Humanist View

Throughout history there have been those logicians—from Socrates to Bertrand Russell—who have branded the Judeo-Christian biblical concept as irrational, antilibertarian, and unenforceable. And logicians do not give up. In their rational broadsides and humanistic manifestos signed by intellectual grandees, they assert the absolute right of the individual to control his or her own bodily destiny in regard to reproduction, medical treatment or lack of it, and termination, including euthanasia and suicide. You can read about humanist views and hear them expressed on the nightly news all the time. Manifesto mongering has made and continues to make an impact. All the more reason for this book, and for those of us who hold to the Judeo-Christian view to speak up.

Biblical Precedents—Individuals Who Experienced Despondency

David, the beloved psalmist, looking down the corridor of the years, had some idea of what might lie ahead for him in his advancing years. This is what he wrote: "Cast me not off in the time of old age; forsake me not when my strength faileth" (Ps. 71:9 KJV).

Did he contemplate suicide? We don't know; the idea isn't mentioned. But we do know that he had great cause for seeking escape, yet he came to his senses time after time. He laid hold upon God's help and cried out: "But I will meditate upon your kindness. . . . Day by day the Lord also pours out his steadfast love upon me, and through the night I sing his songs and pray to God who gives me life. . . . O my soul, don't be discouraged! Don't be upset! Expect God to act. For I know that I shall again have plenty of reason to praise him for all that he will do! He is my help! He is my God!" (Ps. 42:6, 8, 11). David recognized that human life is of value to God even when downcast.

David summed up his thoughts about death and his problems when he said, "For if I die I cannot give you glory by praising you before my friends" (Ps. 6:5).

David had learned what all of us need to understand. We are not promised immunity from periods of despondency, sickness, financial reverses, or problems of one kind or another, regardless of our age. But God is there for us. He is always there to comfort us and make us strong even in our moments of greatest weakness.

Escaping from the Despair That Drives One to Suicide

Moses, Elijah, Paul, David, and many others who have long preceded us discovered that it is always safe to flee to God.

God's comfort can make you strong in weakness. He may not take away your problems; health may not be restored—you may have to live with your medications, your wheelchair, your cane—and God may not remove the cross, but he will give you strength to bear it. He may not remove you from the battle, but he will give peace in the midst of personal war. He does not always remove adversity, but he gives courage to endure. Please hear me. I speak from experience. I have "been there, done that."

When my husband dropped dead in the backyard of our newly built retirement home in northern California, I wasn't sure I could go on, or that I even wanted to. But I did. I moved my focus from the heartache, the loneliness, and the realities that confronted me and turned, as was my habit, to the Word of God. This was not escapism. This was a recognition that the God who formed me, who took me from my widowed mother's womb, who took care of me from birth through all the decades of my life, who had a plan for my life, wasn't about to abandon me. I could trust him with the details. I did.

I remembered much-loved author Joe Bayly's words long years before when he'd heard me speak at a Billy Graham

Decision School of Writing in Minneapolis. Joe had come up to me and kindly said, "Helen, you write with a sob in your throat, don't you?" I looked up at him, tears forming in my eyes, and responded, "It takes one to know one." I tell you this just to say that I know what it means to have a sob in my throat and to feel overwhelmed at times. To you who are despairing, I feel a strong kinship.

A New Vision for the Future

In Dr. Wirt's book, in the "vision of usefulness that Jesus imparted to him," he speaks of this vision as giving old age its splendor, turning wrinkles into smiles, senility into seniority, and slowness of speech into wisdom.

> It can change complaining spirits into prayer warriors. It can suffuse the gradual process of aging with dignity, and so attract the admiration and affection of younger people. Can you imagine what a thrill it is when someone says to you, "When I get old, I would like to be like you"? I am not telling you that old age *ought* to be the best time of your life, but that it *will* be the best. As the vision takes hold of you and gives you direction, God will write a new chapter in your biography—a chapter you never dreamed was possible. You will find that God is a Master Host: He serves dessert. He saves the sweets for the end of the banquet, the best for the last—the last for which the first was made.

How do I know all this? Because God's Word declares it:

> "The righteous will flourish like a palm tree,
> they will grow like a cedar of Lebanon;
> planted in the house of the Lord,
> they will flourish in the courts of our God.

They will still bear fruit in old age,
they will stay fresh and green."
Psalm 92:12–14 NIV, italics added[12]

Someone God used to express thoughts about getting older was Moses, who was in his eighties or older when he wrote Psalm 90. Here the life span of humankind is mentioned, and it is interesting that although the biblical life span of these ancients was, for the most part, considerably longer than ours today, in Psalm 90 it is spoken of like this: "The days of our lives are seventy years; and if by reason of strength they are eighty years, yet . . . it is soon cut off, and we fly away . . . so teach us to number our days, that we may gain a heart of wisdom" (Ps. 90:10–12 NKJV). And the final message of Moses, trudging out there in the desert for forty years, seeing one after another of his fellow sojourners' lives come to an end, are these beautiful words: "And let the beauty of the LORD our God be upon us, and establish the work of our hands for us; yes, establish the work of our hands" (Ps. 90:17 NKJV).

"Take it one day at a time," I tell myself, my children, and others when circumstances threaten to overwhelm. Life is to be a step-by-step walk, not a marathon run. And always remember that the Bible says, "The steps of a good man are ordered by the LORD, and He delights in his way. Though he fall, he shall not be utterly cast down; for the LORD upholds him with His hand. I have been young, and now am old; yet have I not seen the righteous forsaken" (Ps. 37:23–25 NKJV). And when we order those steps aright, we can be assured that God sees our stops as well as our steps. Then we also will know what it is to have the "heart of wisdom" Moses talked about.

❧ 11 ❧

Biblical People Who Expressed the Death Wish

Have courage for the great sorrows of life, and patience for the small ones, and when you have laboriously accomplished your daily task, go to sleep in peace. God is awake.

Victor Hugo

The Bible is contemporary. Its heroes and heroines were very human. Their biographies are instructive for us today. We don't have to apologize for our humanness. As Gert Behanna, a former alcoholic whose all-too-human tendencies led her astray, wrote in her life story, "God must have thought an awful lot of us humans; after all, he came in the flesh!"

Consider these cries: "Lord, take away my life" or "O Lord, take my life from me, for it is better for me to die than to live"

130

or "I am not able to bear all this. . . . It is too heavy for me. . . . Kill me, I pray thee." Perhaps you've anguished in prayer like that, or someone you know has cried out like this. That person may even have ended up a suicide statistic. A look at those who uttered these cries is in order.

Moses

Moses had achieved stupendous things for God and his people, but he carried some heavy burdens on his shoulders. It was he who, physically exhausted, overtaxed by the unremitting daily strain of acting as liaison between God and a nation of two million discontented people, having reached—and, in fact, passed—the limit of physical and emotional endurance, cried out in anguish. "I can't carry this nation by myself! The load is far too heavy! If you are going to treat me like this, please kill me right now; it will be a kindness! Let me out of this impossible situation!" (Num. 11:14–15).

It's not difficult to identify with Moses and how he felt so overwhelmed. Who among us hasn't experienced something similar! His complaints were real, but were they justified? Actually, he wasn't bearing the people alone; God was bearing them and also bearing Moses, but Moses's problem was that he wasn't fully casting himself upon God. Moses had temporary amnesia!

The apostle Peter wrote, "[Cast] all your care upon Him, for He cares for you" (1 Pet. 5:7 NKJV), and we can remember that and be helped. But Moses didn't have the New Testament! What he did have, however, was an awesome face-to-face communication with God (see Num. 12:7–8). Did God scold Moses and make him feel guilty for complaining? Here once again we can see God's incredible patience and understanding of our humanness. God gave Moses instructions about how to deal with the situation that appeared so overwhelming. God will not overburden those who are his own. And I love God's sense of humor, for that's how I see what he said to Moses after the situation was brought under control: "Has the LORD's arm been shortened?" (Num. 11:23 NKJV).

God has a long arm! It extends to you. His ability and power are not limited or inadequate.

What Moses couldn't possibly know was that many, many years of wonderful service for God still lay ahead of him. Did God answer his prayer and kill him? No way!

It is a serious thing when a believer—one who has placed his life in God's hand—is robbed of his desire to live.

Elijah

Look at a lone figure sitting forlornly under a juniper tree out in the wilderness. He had fled for his life. And you must get the picture—he ran a long way (over eighty miles) and, in fact, ran "for his life" (1 Kings 19:3). See him, his robe flapping in the wind. Hot in pursuit, anxious to kill him, were the men sent by Queen Jezebel.

Why had he run? Is this the same man who stood on top of Mount Carmel and defied the 450 prophets of Baal? Is this the man who ordered that a trench be built around an altar and filled with four barrels of water and then cried out to God, "LORD God of Abraham, Isaac, and Israel, let it be known this day that You are God in Israel, and that I am Your servant, and that I have done all these things at Your word. Hear me, O LORD, hear me, that this people may know that You are the LORD God" (1 Kings 18:36–37 NKJV)?

Notice that Elijah recognized that if God didn't do it, it wouldn't get done. This is one of the great prayers of Scripture. It's a prayer we can pray. *Father, show me what to do and how to do it, and then, dear God, you do it so that others will know it is you.*

Elijah was praying for the glory of God. That is what moves the arm of God. It was done. It's as dramatic a story as you can read anywhere. The fire of the Lord fell, consuming not only the sacrifice laid on the altar but also the wood, the stones, and the dust and licking up all the water in the trench. God at work! "Now when all the people saw it, they fell on their faces; and they said, 'The LORD, He is God! The LORD, He is God!'" (1 Kings 18:39 NKJV).

At this juncture, Elijah ordered that all the prophets of Baal be slain. It was a brutal thing to do, but it got rid of the apostasy and the heresy. We may not understand some of what took place in those days, but we must trust that it was what God ordered. It was no small task, but God gave Elijah and his helpers special strength.

It was after this that Elijah, fresh from the most dramatic scene imaginable, where he had been the divine instrument in the hands of God, wilts. Wilts yet runs. He sprawls, exhausted, physically and emotionally depleted, unfit to meet the threats of the raging Queen Jezebel who had sent a message: "You killed my prophets, and now I swear by the gods that I am going to kill you by this time tomorrow night" (1 Kings 19:2).

What would Elijah say to us today—to those of us who sometimes feel so drained that we may even have cried out like the prophet himself did, "I've had enough. . . . Take away my life. I've got to die sometime, and it might as well be now" (1 Kings 19:4)? We can identify with Elijah's fatigue and with the desire to just escape. Elijah has his counterpart in all of us who are so very human; he had a counterpart in the New Testament Peter, who when he took his eyes off the Lord, looked at the waves and began to sink. Elijah lost his courage. Yes, we can identify with that.

I don't know who your enemies are, or if you even have any, but Elijah had an enemy in the most wicked woman in the Bible. He felt he had to get out of her reach. You can criticize him; you can find fault with those who, like me, have attempted suicide or thought suicidal thoughts; you can say Romans 8:28 is in the Bible.

But the prophet was wrung out, worn out, overworked. There was a physical cause for the way he acted. He was so exhausted after that experience at Mount Carmel that he probably could have collapsed right there. He would never have run away from Jezebel if he had not been exhausted. And, actually, he stood quite alone.

There are untold numbers of people worldwide standing for the Lord, upholding the Word of God, not all in pulpits, on the mission field, or in recognized ministries, but faithful servants of God of all ages, in all walks of life. And many of them feel quite alone. I think of the many behind-the-scenes people I've been privileged to meet through the writing and career opportunities that have come my way. Some of them showed signs of weariness in well-doing; some were run down; others felt let down; all possessed sensitive souls, open to being God's people where he had placed them. My heart has gone out to them. I continue to care, as I know they struggle with the inequities of life and the strain of pressing on. The journey of life is too difficult to go it alone. We need a Helper. We have him. God has not left us alone and helpless.

God came to Elijah's rescue. As Elijah lay there in the wilderness, he slept. An angel was sent to minister to him. As Elijah awakened he saw that "by his head was a cake baked on coals, and a jar of water. So he ate and drank, and lay down again. And the angel of the LORD came back the second time, and touched him, and said, 'Arise and eat, because the journey is too great for you'" (1 Kings 19:6–7 NKJV).

In the strength of what the Lord provided, Elijah went on for another forty days and forty nights. God's grace *is* sufficient. We are never lost to the watchful loving care of the Lord when we are his children. God didn't answer Elijah's foolish, passionate request to take his life; God understood. He didn't answer my foolish request either. He had work for Elijah to complete. He had work for me to finish. This book represents some of that work; of that I am fully convinced. And God wants you to finish the course he has planned for you as well. God sustained and encouraged Elijah. He is there to do that for you also.

Jonah

Have you ever said, "I'd rather be dead than alive"? Maybe you haven't gone so far as to actually give voice to such thoughts, but still, something similar may have been lurking in the back of your thinking. If so, you have echoed what Jonah, the prophet who ran away from God, said at one time.

God had given Jonah a difficult assignment, but Jonah forgot that God is with us in these difficult places, and he took off in the opposite direction. Fear took hold of him, and he ran away from the Lord (Jon. 1:1–3). Imagine thinking he could hide from the Lord! Instead of going to Nineveh, he went down to the seaport of Joppa, where he found a ship leaving for Tarshish. When a great storm threatened to send the ship and its passengers to the bottom, Jonah told them to throw him out into the sea, because he knew the terrible storm had come because of him (Jon. 1:12). The picture is one of desperation, with the men battling the raging sea. Jonah battled the elements as the wild waves plunged him to the "bottoms of the mountains that rose from off the ocean floor." "The waters closed above me, the seaweed wrapped itself around my head," he said of the awfulness of his descent into "the yawning jaws of death" (Jon. 2:5–6). And Jonah ended up inside the belly of a great fish.

Now, the interior of a great sea monster is a strange place to have a prayer meeting, but Jonah had a confrontation with God in the ocean's depths. He said something very profound (which he later forgot): "When I had lost all hope, I turned my thoughts once more to the Lord" (Jon. 2:7). And that was it.

Can we learn from Jonah's horrible experience that if we would not run away from God, if we would not take our thoughts off him to begin with, we wouldn't get into such trouble or feel "locked out of life," as Jonah put it (Jon. 2:6)?

The Lord ordered the fish to spit up Jonah on the beach, and it did so three days later. Yuck! But now he was on land again. Miracle of miracles! Then the Lord spoke to him once more. God had told him to go to Nineveh to begin with, and that is what had caused him to take off. Now God issued the same order, telling Jonah he must warn the people of Nineveh of their doom. This time Jonah obeyed and set out to deliver God's message to wicked Nineveh. It was a large city, the capital of the area, with extensive suburbs. It took three days for Jonah to walk around it—its circumference was over twenty-seven miles. This was a great city with walls a hundred feet high and forty feet thick. Historians estimate that at the time of Jonah's call for repentance, its residents numbered 175,000 adults and 120,000 children. Not only was it great in size and importance, but it was great in wickedness, with every kind of immoral debauchery imaginable, idolatry, brutality, luxurious living, godless music, crime, poverty, drunkenness, and cruelty. Does it sound like cities in the world today? We don't know the exact message Jonah proclaimed, but it was powerful!

How did Jonah attract crowds wherever he walked? He wouldn't have had any of the methods or tactics employed today to put on a great evangelistic service. Try to get the picture in focus. Here is this man Jonah, a prophet, who walks from one end of the city to the other without using any gimmicks, celebrities, or well-known singers. Entertainment was not his method. But he was a spectacle to see. A man who has spent three days and three nights in a fish simply cannot come out looking like he did before he was swallowed.

Jesus talked about Jonah. What he said is authentication of the historicity of the book of Jonah. Luke 11:30 tells us that Jesus said that just as Jonah was a "sign to the Ninevites, so also the Son of Man will be to this generation" (NKJV). *The Living Bible* makes it very clear. As the crowd pressed in upon Jesus, he preached to them a sermon: "These are evil times, with evil people. They keep asking for some strange happening in the skies [to prove I am the Messiah], but the only proof I will give them is a miracle like that of Jonah, whose experiences proved to the people of Nineveh that God had sent him. My similar experience will prove that God has sent me to these people."

The late Dr. Harry Rimmer, a much-respected scientist, theologian, and author of many highly sought-after and best-selling books, told of meeting a man who had spent two days inside a fish and lived to tell about it. The man was put on exhibit in a London museum as the "Jonah of the Twentieth Century." Dr. Rimmer explained that the man didn't have a hair on his body, and his skin was a yellowish-iron color. The fish's gastric juices had reacted upon the man as the fish had tried to digest him.[1]

If that happened to a twentieth-century man, it must have happened to Jonah. Jonah looked strange. No doubt about it.

When he stopped at a corner and a crowd gathered, they would ask, "What happened to you? Where have you been?"

Listen! God can use any means he chooses to get the message of the good news of his saving grace out to sinful humanity! Jonah would have replied with the truth of his experience. "I am a walking miracle. I am as a man from the dead. A fish swallowed me because God asked me to come here and warn you people of your wicked ways and what will happen to you, and I tried to run away from him to Tarshish." Did the people ridicule him? No way! They listened. "Forty days from now Nineveh will be destroyed!" (Jon. 3:5). Everyone from the king and his nobles on down believed Jonah, covered themselves with sackcloth, sat in ashes, and turned from their evil ways.

Hear what the Bible tells us: "When God saw that they had put a stop to their evil ways, he abandoned his plan to destroy them, and didn't carry it through" (Jon. 3:10).

God gives us choices—we can ignore God's Word, or we can accept it, turn to him, and be saved. When people reject his Word, turn from him, scoff, and ridicule, they are lost. But God will always save when there is repentance, a sorrow for sin, and a turning to him. That was the effect Jonah's message had on the people of Nineveh.

Yet what was its effect on the messenger? This is where Jonah's desire to end it all comes into focus. One wishes this didn't have to be seen, yet it is in the Word of God for a reason. Maybe that reason includes you or someone you know who needs to hear this. Instead of leaping for joy, praising and thanking God, what did Jonah do? He became angry. He complained to God:

> "This is exactly what I thought you'd do, Lord, when I was there in my own country and you first told me to come here.

That's why I ran away to Tarshish. For I knew you were a gracious God, merciful, slow to get angry, and full of kindness; I knew how easily you could cancel your plans for destroying these people.

"Please kill me, Lord; I'd rather be dead than alive [when nothing that I told them happens]."

Then the Lord said, "Is it right to be angry about this?"

Jonah 4:2–4

Jonah went outside the city and made a leafy shelter to shade himself as he waited to see if anything might still happen to the city. When the leaves of the shelter withered in the heat, he was even more angry. God took pity upon him and arranged a vine, a gourd, to grow up quickly so its broad leaves could provide shade. Jonah sat under the gourd, still watchful to see what, if anything, would happen to Nineveh. Day after day he watered the gourd—after all, it was providing shade, and he was glad for it. But a worm came along and ate the gourd, and it died.

Jonah sat there sulking, moaning, and feeling sorry for himself, because it was very hot, his shade had died, and he grew faint and wished to die. There are those who believe that this second time Jonah might have experienced something physical, such as sunstroke, that might have left him sick enough to wish for death. "Then he wished death for himself, and said, 'It is better for me to die than to live'" (Jon. 4:8 NKJV). Moreover, his predictions weren't coming true, and he felt like a fool.

God once again said to Jonah, "Is it right for you to be angry about the plant?" (Jon. 4:9 NKJV).

"Yes," Jonah said, "it is; it is right for me to be angry enough to die!" (Jon. 4:9).

"Then the Lord said, 'You feel sorry for yourself when your shelter is destroyed, though you did no work to put it there, and it is, at best, short-lived. And why shouldn't I feel sorry for a great city like Nineveh with its 120,000 people in utter spiritual darkness?'" (Jon. 4:10–11). (The reference to 120,000 people is to children who weren't yet old enough to know their right hand from their left. This is the widely held understanding of this numerical reference. The NKJV says, "And should I not pity Nineveh, that great city, in which are more than one hundred and twenty thousand persons who cannot discern between their right hand and their left?")

What happened to Jonah after this? I like to think he was sorry for his outbursts and asked God to forgive him. I like to think that he went back and walked the streets of Nineveh again, this time gathering groups of people together and instructing them about God's mercy, grace, and love. That's what those of us who have experienced God's mercy—his forgiveness and love—ourselves should be doing. Everyone needs hope. Hope for today, hope for the future. We can help others receive that.

🕯12🕯

A Savage Enemy

This terrible illness colors everything—a family cannot escape.

An anonymous woman whose family has been impacted by the mental illness of a loved one

Mental illness strikes one in five Americans each year. More than half of those who need treatment do not get it, either because they do not seek it or because they do not have access to it. Lack of access has driven far too many of our most vulnerable population out into the streets, jails, and prisons. Mental illness can affect anyone, and few families are untouched by mental health problems. The results can be devastating and lead to a diminished quality of life, poverty, unemployment, and homelessness. This is according to the report on mental health by the surgeon general of the United States.

Suicide is a potential danger in those who have schizophrenia, the most complex, extremely puzzling condition, the most chronic and disabling of all the major mental illnesses. People with schizophrenia appear to have a higher rate of suicide than the general population. These facts are released by the Schizophrenia Research Branch of the National Institute of Mental Health, which states that nearly three million Americans will develop schizophrenia during the course of their lives, and about a hundred thousand schizophrenia patients are in public mental hospitals on any given day. The treatments available for schizophrenia, while very important in relieving at least some of the suffering for many of the people affected, are not yet preventing the common pattern of repeated relapse with chronic disabilities in social and occupational functioning. Schizophrenia remains poorly understood and largely feared by the public.[1]

A Day of Infamy

National attention was riveted on the attempted assassination of the president on March 30, 1981. The date has gone down in history as a day of infamy—the day John W. Hinckley Jr., the youngest of Jack and Jo Ann Hinckley's children, tried to assassinate Ronald Reagan. Life for those parents has never been the same. This tragedy revealed that their son was schizophrenic.

"Devastating"

E. Fuller Torrey, M.D., in *Surviving Schizophrenia: A Family Manual*, explained that schizophrenia is a devastating illness not only for the afflicted person but for the person's family as well. It was his opinion that there is probably no disease, including cancer, that causes more anguish. "Of all types of handicapping conditions in adults, chronic schizophrenia probably gives rise to the most difficulties at home."[2]

Ask the family who has been there, family members who live with the ever-present knowledge that someone dear to them is a victim. I've talked to a number of such families. I know a mother whose three daughters are schizophrenic. "Totally devastating," she says. *Devastating* is the word you will hear time after time when talking to family members whose loved ones have this mental illness.

Tad Bartimus with the *Associated Press* interviewed a typical middle-class family whose son is a paranoid schizophrenic. The mother of this adult son said schizophrenia is a disease worse than cancer. "When you get cancer of the body, either somebody cuts it out or you take medicine or treatments to get rid of it. You either get well or eventually die. . . . Eric's illness will just go on and on and on. There is no real hope for us. . . . Those of us who have a schizophrenic in our family, who love a chronically mentally ill person, are on a constant roller coaster. We go up, down, up, down. We are either grasping at the merest shred of hope, the slightest possibility of improvement, or we are floundering in despair."

From Eric's anguished father came these words: "None of it is his fault. He's sick. There's something haywire in his brain." Eric's parents and other family members are but a single filament in a large web of Americans whose lives are in financial and emotional turmoil because someone close to them is mentally ill.

I have a friend in northern California whose brilliant twenty-three-year-old son, newly graduated from college, all set to make a name for himself in his chosen profession, was, to all appearances, taken from them—and from himself—when

143

he disappeared into the never-never land of schizophrenia. He was still around physically, but mentally he was gone. It happened more than thirty years ago. "He's been institutionalized five times, and then is placed in halfway houses," she told me on a recent visit. "We had to give up our hopes, dreams, and aspirations for our son." I got to know her son when we lived in the small town where Ben (not his real name) would sit at the counter in the country café, the favorite meeting place for many locals. Everyone knew him; everyone treated him with respect. One day I deduced that the gracious gray-haired woman who came alongside him was his mother. After that she and I became friends.

"Chronic Sorrow"

I came to recognize what is often called the "chronic sorrow" that family members experience. Eventually, but not always, there may come acceptance, but there is never closure. Alternating periods of relapse and remission make up the roller-coaster existence for all concerned. Uncertainty marks the future. One is never certain when socially inappropriate or disruptive behavior will occur. Family members feel humiliated and ashamed.

When someone you love—a daughter or a son—is married to a mentally ill person, the in-laws also become part of the devastation. Then if there are children born into the family of a schizophrenic, the nightmare of mental illness is compounded. Always, in the back of everyone's mind, is the thought, *What if this child has inherited the genetic tendency?* Children over the age of five can develop schizophrenia, but it is very rare before adolescence. More research is needed to clarify the relationship of schizophrenia occurring in childhood to that occurring in adolescence and adulthood. The first psychotic symptoms of schizophrenia are often seen in the teens or twenties in men and in the twenties or early thirties in women.

If you are a grandparent whose grandchild has grown up in a home with a schizophrenic mother or father, the anguish and uncertainty about what is taking place is always there. When the grandchild becomes a young adult and adult-onslaught schizophrenia hits, grandparents find themselves caught in an agonizing emotional tailspin. Hopes are dashed.

The home life of the mentally ill is often reflected in poor living habits, household disarray, and always social stigma, making it difficult, if not impossible, to have friends over or for the children to invite their friends in. Where there are children, the burden of many of the homemaking responsibilities falls to them, especially when the father is working and it is the mother who is ill.

The parentification of such children is a reality. The stigma of having a mentally ill parent is something they always have to deal with. They are robbed of their childhood. A brother or sister may also be diagnosed with the illness. Some siblings manage with tremendous effort to keep themselves afloat in the sea of confusion that exists in the home. If grandparents, aunts or uncles, friends, or some support system such as a church lift the children's heads above water periodically, they serve as a sort of life-support system. But such homes are usually characterized by chaos and disorder. It is incredibly sad for siblings. Usually there will be traumatic episodes involving bizarre and frightening behavior, and the home becomes a war zone. Many siblings, however, go on to live productive, successful lives with great empathy and capacity for caring for others that is exemplary and beautiful to observe.

Often schizophrenics are medically noncompliant. That is, they don't want to take their medication and will become very agitated about it. Imagine being the husband or wife of the ill person and having to handle this every day. When such marriages survive, it is to the credit of the well person. One husband told me, "I took the vow, 'until death do us part,' and 'for better or for worse, in sickness and in health,' and I will take care of her."

The Grief of Mental Illness

When the psychiatric diagnosis is made, there is grief and mourning—the stages of loss that accompany the normal loss of a loved one through death. With a loved one who has mental illness, mourning may be a longer process as those concerned learn to adapt, cope with, and accept the loss and move on, but still never with final closure. The illness is just something that exists; it's there, like a dull ache. These stages of grief affect not only the family caregivers but also the individuals themselves.

Dealing with the grief of mental illness is about acceptance, but it is also about advocacy and self-help groups. There are many who do not know that mental illness is a brain disorder treatable with medications and other treatments. Schizophrenia, bipolar disorder, and major depression—these are neurological illnesses just as multiple sclerosis, epilepsy, and Alzheimer's are. In talking to an in-law about this, I pointed out that medication is to schizophrenia as insulin is to diabetes or heart medicine is to heart disease. But one of the problems with the mentally ill is that they do not want to see themselves as sick people, so there is denial. They resent supervision and being told to take medication. Dr. Torrey, in *Surviving Schizophrenia*, says reasoning with a schizophrenic is like trying to bail out the ocean with a bucket.

Many people wonder about mental illness and ask questions like these:

Are individuals born with schizophrenia or with the predisposition to some form of mental illness? Is it genetic and hereditary? Yes, genetic factors produce a vulnerability to schizophrenia. It has long been known that schizophrenia runs in families. Children of a schizophrenic parent each have about a 10 percent chance of developing the illness.

Can people with schizophrenia function in society? Yes, if they follow the outlined course of treatment and have some degree of supervision by a family member or friend to make certain they take the drugs. The problem is that schizophrenic patients frequently become ill during the critical trade-learning or career-forming years of life—ages eighteen to thirty-five—so they are less likely to complete the training required for skilled work. As a result, many schizophrenic patients not only suffer thinking and emotional difficulties but lack social and work skills as well.

Are they a danger to themselves and others? Uncontrolled, they can be, but there is general agreement among professionals that most violent crimes are not committed by schizophrenic persons. More typically, schizophrenics prefer to withdraw and be left alone. Some acutely disturbed patients may become physically violent or do something irrational like John Hinckley Jr. did.

Is anything new being discovered to help the mentally ill? Yes, there are new and improved medications and antipsychotic drugs. Also, some communities provide rehabilitation programs that emphasize social and vocational training.

Torrey called schizophrenics the lepers of the twentieth century, but that attitude extends into the twenty-first century as well. We hear and read about street people, those doing bizarre things in city after city, those whose families and friends have turned their backs on them or who have given up or who themselves have just taken off. Perhaps you've seen

An Eclipse of the Soul

them along the highways with their cardboard signs, in dirty, ragged clothes, drifting alone from ugly rooming houses to ramshackle apartments, often in a state of near starvation. Or they will make their way into city missions where they are fed, given a change of clothing and an opportunity to shower, and provided with a bed. It is believed that only about half of this country's chronically mentally ill have the benefit of family support and care. Coping with psychotic behavior is emotionally, financially, and physically draining. Not all families are up to it.[3] One doctor says, "The single biggest advance in coping with schizophrenia since the introduction of antipsychotic drugs has been the advent of family support groups."

One sibling related, "I see my brother in every disheveled and disoriented homeless person."

Some years ago my husband and I transported one such person from our community to another about an hour away. He explained that he'd been released from a Florida jail and had made his way to California. Now he wandered from place to place, from one church to another, seeking handouts, some sort of safety, comfort, and help. He found help at our church, my husband being the associate pastor at the time. As he sat in the backseat of our car conversing, we realized that he was a mentally disturbed young man. We stopped at a restaurant and urged him to order anything on the menu that he wanted. He was ravenous. He was in his late twenties, he told us, and said he hadn't been with his family in a long time.

"They don't want me," he said, his voice edged with sorrow. After we left him, I cried much of the way home. Many of these people, thrust out into society, tend to drift away, losing contact with family and friends. Afraid to seek mental health care, they often run afoul of the criminal court system. One psychiatrist working with the Los Angeles County Department of Mental Health said he had never seen a more victimized part of the population in his life.

What about Suicide among Schizophrenics?

My research reveals that the feelings of hopelessness that often accompany the illness lead to suicidal thoughts or suicide attempts in as many as half of all schizophrenia patients. The long-term risk of suicide among these people is estimated to be 10 to 13 percent, a rate approaching that in mood disorders.[4]

A National Disgrace: The Criminalization of Mental Illness

Joseph Walsh, Ph.D., an associate professor of social work at Virginia Commonwealth University in Richmond, says he was surprised to learn that between 1955 and 1985 the annual national state hospital population fell by two-thirds, but the number of persons with mental illness in jails rose by 150 percent. Right there is a picture of what has too long been happening, with jails persisting as sites of incarceration for persons with mental illness.

Family members may be successful in advocating for some improvements in their local criminal justice systems, particularly jails, because these are under local governmental control. The voices of family members can be instrumental in helping law enforcement personnel, as well as mental health professionals, make policy decisions that will promote a more coordinated local system of care. Sheriffs, jail administrators, and jails are not well suited to care for persons with mental illness, as they were never designed for that purpose. When a relative is in jail, the most effective professional resources are likely to be found at the public community services agency, and the detainee's immediate needs will best be met if family members seek such help right away. Family advocacy groups, including the Alliance for the Mentally Ill and the Mental Health Association, have demonstrated a positive impact in this regard in some states.

The situation of the mentally ill in this country is a national disgrace. Researchers call it the "criminalization of mental illness" and "transinstitutionalization"—the movement of people with serious mental illness from community psychiatric hospitals into jails and prisons. Walsh points out that there is an estimated 35 to 55 percent lifetime arrest rate for persons with serious mental illnesses, even though less than one-fifth of them are ever convicted of a crime. Between 6 and 15 percent of all persons in jails have a mental illness. Their common offenses include simple assault, theft, robbery, shoplifting, alcohol- or drug-related charges, trespassing, and "failure to appear" court warrants. Homeless persons are overrepresented among these detainees. The special problems faced by persons with mental illness in jail include mistreatment by other inmates, the negative effects of isolation or overcrowding, unmet needs for medications and other mental health services, and jail resource shortages regarding treatment information and referral services.

One advocate for people with mental illness says, "We have a new community mental health system, it's called jail." She points to the beginning of the "deinstitutionalization" in the 1970s, when psychiatric hospitals across the nation were forced to downsize drastically, resulting in hundreds of thousands of mentally ill people being forced into communities that did not have enough supportive systems to give these people a real shot at living. "The incarceration of thousands of people with serious mental illness is having tragic consequences nationwide; a

Department of Justice report, issued in July 1999, found that about 16 percent of jail and prison inmates nationwide have mental illness—a total of over a quarter million incarcerated mentally ill Americans."[5]

This is too large a problem to do justice to in a book such as this. At best, I can only point out the problem and urge that you become better informed through more reading and research. But it is time for us as Christians to speak out and do something once we have learned more. When we look at Jesus, we see that he was always an advocate for the down-trodden, the depressed, those with obvious mental illness, those needing help, hope, and healing. The church—that's people like you and me—must do more than teach about these things, for the church's primary task is to be the people of God. In the next chapter I'll point out some ways we can be "gatekeepers."

Evil, Crazy, Demon Possessed, Postpartum Depressed, or Severely Mentally Ill?

When Andrea Yates, a young mother of five in Houston, Texas, was sentenced to life in prison for killing her children by drowning, the public's awareness of postpartum depression (PPD) came front and center. The horrific account was chilling. Carol Steiker, a professor at Harvard Law School, was cited in *Newsweek*'s initial story as saying, "What can we say about a mom who kills her five kids? She's got to be evil, or she's got to be crazy," giving voice to what people around the world were saying. The account went on to say that thanks in large part to highly publicized cases like Yates's, awareness of PPD is growing. But when such an illness results in infanticide, the American public has trouble being sympathetic. The agony of this tragedy will remain with Russell Yates, the husband and father, for the rest of his life, even as it will with Andrea herself. Family members and friends will never quite be the same. It was horrendous. Monstrous, perverse, unthinkable. Some labeled it cold-blooded madness. Others said she had to have been demon possessed, that she was controlled by evil spirits.

There have been other cases of postpartum disorders resulting in mothers killing their children and often themselves. One Indiana jury convicted Judy Kirby, age thirty-one, of killing seven people (including three of her children) when she crashed her Pontiac Firebird into a minivan while driving at high speed in the wrong direction. Judy was the mother of eight children, including a five-month-old, who had a long family history of paranoid schizophrenia and had, in fact, been hospitalized for "a major depressive disorder with psychotic features," according to one of her attorneys. She was sentenced to 215 years behind bars.

The *Newsweek* story also told of Melanie Stokes, a forty-one-year-old mother who gave birth to a much-wanted baby girl, Sommer Skyy, but who became despondent after the delivery. She was treated, but according to her mother, Carol Blocker, it was too little too late. Melanie jumped to her death from the ledge of a Days Inn just three months after delivery. Mrs. Blocker feels more hospital time might have saved her daughter.

The "baby blues," a temporary period of weepiness that up to 80 percent of new mothers undergo, is very real, but PPD goes beyond that and is characterized by persistent feelings of anxiety, hopelessness, guilt, insomnia, lack of motivation, and sometimes thoughts or fantasies of harming oneself or even the baby. Doctors estimate that between 5 and 20 percent of all new mothers suffer from it. A much smaller number, however—about one woman in a thousand—experience the far more severe symptoms of postpartum psychosis, which goes beyond PPD. It is said that PPD rarely results in the kind of tragedy that unfolded in Houston with Andrea Yates. But in postpartum psychosis, there are hallucinations, paranoia, and delusional, suicidal, or homicidal thoughts.

One can only hope that the Andrea Yates tragedy, as well as the stories of others, will now be a huge wake-up call and that postpartum depression and the possibility of postpartum psychosis will never again be taken lightly by anyone. Andrea had attempted suicide in June 1999 by overdosing on pills prescribed for her ailing father. According to Russell Yates, his wife's depression returned with a vengeance within a few months of the birth of her fifth child, little Mary, triggered or at least aggravated by the death of her father. "She just went spiraling down" and never responded well to medications. "She became robotic," he said, and showed "nervous habits." *Newsweek* reported that "it is hard to conceive of the snakes that were writhing in her head."[6]

Which brings us back to what was mentioned earlier—those who feel Andrea Yates was possessed by evil spirits. Neil T. Anderson, in *The Bondage Breaker*, raises the question that if dark spiritual powers are no longer attacking believers, why would Paul alert us to them and insist that we arm ourselves against them? (See Eph. 6:12–13.) To wrestle against dark spiritual forces is not just a first-century phenomenon. Anderson states, "It is important to understand that demonic influence is not an external force in the physical realm; it is the internal manipulation of the central nervous system."[7] The powers and forces that Paul wrote about in the first century are still evident in the twenty-first century.

Jesus encountered evil spirits wherever he went. The Gospels tell of how he responded—he delivered individuals from evil spirits; he healed them. Demonic control over vulnerable individuals is real. Jesus is the bondage breaker; he alone can set anyone free. As Christians, we are in a war, but it is winnable. Let us use our freedom in Christ to alert others. Let us appropriate that freedom for ourselves. I referred to the apostle Peter's warning before, but it needs repeating here: "Your adversary, the devil, prowls around like a roaring lion, seeking someone to devour. But resist him, firm in your faith" (1 Pet. 5:8–9 NASB). When Satan and his demonic influence are confronted by God's authority, Satan has to go.

Evil was on the prowl in the Yateses' Houston home. Spiritual forces of wickedness are a present-day reality (see Eph. 6:12). I leave it to experts like Neil Anderson to address this subject in depth.

A Ray of New Hope

Dr. Crystal Blyler, a social science analyst at the U.S. Department of Health and Human Services Substance Abuse and Mental Health Services Administration and a schizophrenia researcher, says that advances in knowledge about schizophrenia, its treatment, and the effective community support services now available offer a great deal of hope to people diagnosed with this disorder.

"Studies have shown that, with the right support, a substantial degree of recovery from schizophrenia is possible."[8] Dr. Blyler points to media documentation of numerous examples of successful people with schizophrenia and an active consumer movement that provides prominent role models.

But schizophrenia *is* different from other types of problems faced by those with severe and persistent mental illness, and schizophrenics are more likely than people with other psychological disorders (e.g., depression, anxiety disorders) to fall into the severe and persistent category. They are more likely to need lifelong mental health care, to experience repeated or long-term psychiatric hospitalizations, and to need to fall under legal guardianship as adults.[9]

Neil Anderson believes that terms like *schizophrenia*, *paranoia*, and *psychosis* are labels classifying symptoms. He asks, what or who is causing the symptoms? Is it a neurological or hormonal problem, or perhaps a chemical imbalance? Certainly these possibilities must be explored. "But what if no physical cause is found? Then it must be a psychological problem. But which school of psychology do you choose: biblical or secular? And why isn't someone exploring the possibility that the problem is primarily spiritual?"[10]

Dr. Anderson raises an important issue, and if indeed no physical cause for your or your loved one's mental health problems is found, then give serious thought to the need to address the issue of the influence of the spirit world. To seek help from a Christian counselor who understands the activities of Satan would be very wise.

Recovery for Families

Chris Amenson, Ph.D., director of Pacific Clinics Institute and clinical instructor in the UCLA Department of Psychiatry and Biobehavioral Sciences, points out that newly discovered medications, cognitive and rehabilitation therapies, and vocational programs offer a hope for recovery for mentally ill individuals that was unheard of ten years ago. "Every day, I see NAMI [National Association for Mental Illness] families give their negative feelings a place, and then use their energy to do incredible, courageous things that make life better for us all."[11]

For those whose families have been impacted by mental illness, whatever the clinical diagnosis—if, in fact, the problem is physical—seek out the support that can be found in organizations such as the nonprofit National Association for Mental Illness (NAMI). (See appendix A for helpful information about NAMI and other resources.) Everyone I know who has been challenged by mental illness within their family tells me of the ongoing help and group support this organization and others like it provide. To increase one's network of resources through awareness is of major importance. To be solution oriented, not problem oriented, is to focus one's energy, resources, and time so that one can more effectively care for the family member with the illness, the other family members, and oneself.

✿13✿

The Role of Gatekeepers

God alone understands the state of mind of those who end
their own lives. . . . Don't be surprised if you find yourself
wanting to avoid religious people, the church, the Bible, or
even God Himself. Emotional pain can put distance between
ourselves and others.

Martin R. De Haan, president, RBC Ministries

I picked up on the term *gatekeepers* from Dr. Norman L.
Farberow, at one time Los Angeles clinical psychologist
and cofounder of the Los Angeles Suicide Prevention
Center. He stressed that suicidal people are made, not born.
In order to unmake them, suicidal behaviorists and gatekeepers must learn more about the roots of self-destructive
behavior and the various things these beginnings foster.
"The language of crisis is filled with unexpected twists and
turns," he stated.

So gatekeepers can be persons who are not professionals in the field of mental health but who are likely to meet people who are suicidal. "These would be police, clergymen, lawyers or teachers. A large part of our effort is aimed at these groups. The goal is to educate them to not draw back in horror if someone professes to be suicidal. The gatekeepers can help by being *concerned* and by *trying* to help,"[1] according to Farberow. I see gatekeepers also as informed, concerned, compassionate Christians and, of course, family members.

Gatekeepers at suicide prevention centers seek, through crisis intervention, to stop people from killing themselves. All callers are dealt with in a gentle, kind way. The objective is to establish rapport with the caller so he or she doesn't feel alone. "We let the caller know that we're interested, concerned, expert, and that we can help. We communicate this quickly by the questions we ask," Dr. Farberow explained.

The primary task is to help the person survive through the immediate time of crisis. By getting the individual to talk, the phone counselor gets into the details of the event or circumstances that kicked off the crisis and is then better able to convey the impression that he or she understands what's been happening in the depths of the caller's misery. The approach is to develop rapport and a plan for treatment on the phone. If the suicidal person is completely chaotic, disorganized, and confused, with all kinds of problems weighing in at once, then information must be extracted from the caller so help can be dispatched and the telephone counselor can determine the best plan of action.

About 60 percent of callers are suicidal themselves; the other 40 percent are family members or friends of a suicidal person, seeking counsel, advice, and help. In summary, the role of a gatekeeper volunteer is this: (1) to establish a relationship (rapport) with the caller, (2) to clarify the problem,

(3) to evaluate the caller's suicide potential, (4) to assess the caller's strengths and weaknesses, (5) to formulate a plan of therapy or help, and (6) to mobilize resources.

The Role of the Church in Providing Gatekeepers

The church can encourage individuals to be gatekeepers. It could urge its people to become a part of local suicide prevention centers, mental health agencies, or organizations where volunteers are needed—and the need always exists.

Beyond this, the church could utilize the concerned caregivers in its midst, providing an opportunity for them to be gatekeepers. An example of such work is that provided by the Crystal Cathedral in Garden Grove, California (known especially for its television program, *Hour of Power*, and the dynamic ministry of Dr. Robert Schuller). An ongoing effort is made to provide counseling to individuals who need such help through Crystal Cathedral's New Hope Crisis Counseling Center twenty-four-hour hotline. In addition, support and grief counseling are provided, along with a New Hope Crisis Counseling Center teenline. (See appendix A.)

The point is that not only *could* churches be doing this, but they *should* be. And thankfully, many are in one way or another taking seriously what the Word of God says about extending ourselves to the needy. There is a dimension to despair, suffering, loneliness, and mental illness that calls for a deep, caring willingness on the part of Christ's followers to move into the space occupied by those who hurt with practical help and love that goes beyond words—to become gatekeepers.

It has been pointed out that if the church commits itself to being a community of truth in which its members can dare to tell the truth about their lives and where its members are willing to hear the stories of pain, suffering, and failure of others, it can then confront in love even the most difficult situations and crises, including suicide.

If the church also will commit itself to being a community of love, not quick to judge, then its members would feel safe and comfortable placing themselves at the disposal of, for instance, a team ministry to whom the wounded and the hurting, troubled survivors of a suicide could turn in their distress.

And if the church is committed to being a community of joy where new life in Christ is celebrated—and such news gets around a community—then those who are in need of help will come and receive what is needed.[2]

The Question Everyone Wonders About

Is suicide unforgivable? If a Christian takes his or her own life, is he or she condemned? Did he or she go to heaven? Whatever form the question takes, the idea—usually left unsaid—is whether or not the suicide victim can be forgiven and is with the Lord.

Speaking very bluntly—and certainly this is not something I like to recall—I can tell you that my last thought before gulping the sleeping pills was, *God, forgive me. I'd rather be with you.* So who am I, who are you, to pass judgment on a suicide victim? Do we know what that person's last thoughts were? Some will say, "Oh, but that thought preceded the act. The person cannot be forgiven, because he couldn't have repented of doing it." Do you commit sins you don't even recognize as overt sins? At the moment of death, has everyone named and repented of *all* their sins? What about the person killed in an accident—a plane or car crash, a train accident, a fatal fall? The futility of trying to answer such questions is obvious.

There was a time when suicide was blamed on momentary insanity, so the idea was passed along that God wouldn't hold such a person accountable even though it was a sinful act. I heard this explanation when a neighbor hanged herself when I was a little girl. Temporary insanity is a possible explanation, but people who are not insane self-destruct. For most suicides, there is tunnel vision (see also chapter 5). The suicidal person fails to see beyond his or her present pain, and he or she does the unthinkable. The late Dr. Lewis Smedes, professor emeritus of theology and ethics at Fuller Theological Seminary in Pasadena, California, puts it very well: "[Most] people who take their own lives are not usually cool and rational about it. Nor do they mean to flout the will of God. Most of the . . . people who attempt suicide every year in America do not so much choose death as stumble down into it from a steep slope of despair."[3]

Is there a biblical basis for believing that Jesus will welcome home a believer who died at his or her own hands? Dr. Smedes pointed to Romans 8:38–39, that neither life nor death can separate the believer from the love of God in Christ Jesus. Jesus died for *all* our sins—if indeed he reckons suicide always as sin.

> I believe that, as Christians, we should worry less about whether Christians who have killed themselves go to heaven, and worry more about how we can help people like them find hope and joy in living. Our most urgent problem is not the morality of suicide but the spiritual and mental despair that drag people down into it.
>
> Loved ones who have died at their own hands we can safely trust to our gracious God. Loved ones whose spirits are even now slipping so silently toward death, these are *our* burden.[4]

This points again to the need for gatekeepers.

"In the Dark Corridors of Human Experience . . ."

In responding to the question a father asked about whether those who end their own lives could go to heaven, Martin De Haan had said, "Yes, those who take their own lives can go to heaven. Our last choice in this life does not determine where we go after death." But then he heard the rest of the man's story from a mutual friend. This father was uncertain about where his son was in his spiritual journey, and he was unable to further talk about his loss with De Haan. Later, writing in *Times of Discovery*, the newsletter of the TV broadcast ministry of *Day of Discovery*, De Haan further responded:

> I'd never wish your pain or loss on anyone. Yet this I'm sure of. If it were possible, you could find strength and endurance in a face-to-face conversation with the wisest and most loving Person who ever lived. Even if He didn't answer all of your questions, you would hear words that would give you the courage you need to live the rest of your life in a way that would honor the memory of your son. It is when our broken hearts drive us to the place where we wonder if we can continue that we have every reason to cling to the One who loves better than we do. He is the One who says, "Come to Me, all you who are weary and burdened, and I will give you rest."[5]

De Haan talked about Jesus voluntarily laying aside the boundless understanding he shared with his Father and walking through the dark corridors of human experience. In all his life here on earth, although quite short in duration, Jesus showed that he trusted the unseen hand of God, and he has left us with the record of that brief sojourn here so that we can be comforted, helped, and encouraged to keep on keeping on.

162

⚘14⚘

Never Give Up!

Do yourself no harm.

The apostle Paul,
Acts 16:28 NKJV

In Acts 16:22–40 we see Paul and his companion Silas imprisoned in Philippi. Roman custom dictated that the prison jailer was responsible for his prisoners. The jailer was threatened with death if the prisoners escaped, so taking no chances, he put them into the inner dungeon and clamped their feet into the stocks. Paul and Silas had been stripped and beaten with wooden whips. Again and again the rods slashed down across their bared backs. While the two were in this condition, and were praying and singing praises to God, suddenly there was a great earthquake, the prison was shaken to its foundations, all the doors flew open, and the chains of every prisoner fell off! On today's Richter scale, this earthquake would have had a magnitude of at least a six.

Startled from his sleep, the jailer was panic-stricken. The cell doors were open. The prisoners, he presumed, had all fled. After all, if your chains were loosed, you would run for your life, right? Now *his* life would be on the line. His reaction was characteristic of a Roman soldier—he would rather be dead than incur what would be meted out to him. He stood there, poised, ready to fall on his own sword.

Where were Paul and Silas? Still there! Seeing what was about to happen and the jailer's confusion and fear, Paul loudly called, "Do yourself no harm, for we are all here" (v. 28 NKJV).

Paul stopped a man from taking his life.

What does the Bible have to say to a person who is in the midst of an earthquake experience? God is not an absentee omnipotent who can't be bothered with the cries of despairing people. To the panic-stricken and fearful the answer comes: "Don't do it. Do yourself no harm!" It is a hopeful answer to those who are ready to give up. Paul would tell you, "Never give up! Suicide is not the way out of your plight."

Life Is Good

Although the apostle's writings are liberally sprinkled with exhortations not to despair or succumb to testings, the word *suicide* itself is not mentioned. But the teaching that God-given life is a mystery and a gift to be cherished is prominent.

At the outset of creation, the Bible records that God saw everything he had made and it was "excellent in every way"

(Gen. 1:31). Other translations say it was suitable, fitting, pleasant, very good—God completely approved of what had been made. This is a thesis that has stood the test of time. *Life is good.* We must not despair of its possibilities even though sometimes our circumstances appear very dismal. Situations change. People change.

Paul's words resound with understanding and ring loudly with hope—just as his words to the jailer were convincingly loud. What were some of the things Paul endured?

> To this very hour we have gone hungry and thirsty, without even enough clothes to keep us warm. We have been kicked around without homes of our own. We have worked wearily with our hands to earn our living. We have blessed those who cursed us. We have been patient with those who injured us. We have replied quietly when evil things have been said about us. Yet right up to the present moment we are like dirt under foot, like garbage.
>
> 1 Corinthians 4:11–13

Talk about circumstances that would make you want to give up. So how did Paul handle it?

> But this perishable treasure—this light and power that now shine within us—is held in a perishable container, that is, in our weak bodies. Everyone can see that the glorious power within must be from God and is not our own.
>
> We are pressed on every side by troubles, but not crushed and broken. We are perplexed because we don't know why things happen as they do, but we don't give up and quit. We are hunted down, but God never abandons us. We get knocked down, but we get up again and keep going. These bodies of ours are constantly facing death just as Jesus did; so it is clear to all that it is only the living Christ within [who keeps us safe].

Yes, we live under constant danger to our lives because we serve the Lord, but this gives us constant opportunities to show forth the power of Jesus Christ within our dying bodies. Because of our preaching we face death, but it has resulted in eternal life for you. . . .

That is why we never give up. Though our bodies are dying, our inner strength in the Lord is growing every day. These troubles and sufferings of ours are, after all, quite small and won't last very long. Yet this short time of distress will result in God's richest blessing upon us forever and ever! So we do not look at what we can see right now, the troubles all around us, but we look forward to the joys in heaven which we have not yet seen. The troubles will soon be over, but the joys to come will last forever.

2 Corinthians 4:7–12, 16–18

Can we begin to imagine what the apostle Paul suffered in order to get the gospel out to as many people as possible? It was he who evangelized Asia Minor. He brought a message that withered the Roman Empire. But it was not without a price. He willingly paid for it with his own suffering. And we think we have it bad!

How easily we forget that what we have came to us by way of the kind of things Paul wrote about. And not just Paul—many of the early Christians, including the disciples and followers of Jesus and the first-century believers, were martyred for the faith.

To Keep On Keeping On

We live in a grimly depersonalized world. So did Paul. Did he ever even vaguely express the death wish? Well, yes, but not in the way you might think. He said he never wanted to do anything that would cause him to be ashamed of himself and that he always wanted to be an honor to Christ, whether he lived or whether he died.

> For to me, living means opportunities for Christ, and dying—well, that's better yet! But if living will give me more opportunities to win people to Christ, then I really don't know which is better, to live or die! Sometimes I want to live and at other times I don't, for I long to go and be with Christ. How much happier for me than being here! But the fact is that I can be of more help to you by staying!
>
> Philippians 1:21–24

He thought about death. Don't we all? And if we don't, shouldn't we be giving some consideration to our future destiny? But Paul looked forward to death not just as a release from life's hardships; his focus was on Christ and getting to be with him one day. So he was able to look away from his discomforts, the threats on his life, the physical infirmity that he described as a "thorn in the flesh," and the uncertainties that surrounded his existence. In so doing, he could keep on keeping on.

So Paul's counsel to those to whom he spoke and in the letters he wrote was to keep one's focus where it belongs—on Christ.

His counsel also was that we who are strong are to extend ourselves to others if someone is going through great anguish and grief, if his or her problems loom as too high and insurmountable. Unless such as these receive help from others so that some hope can be infused into them, they may be "swallowed up with too much sorrow" (2 Cor. 2:7 NKJV).

Those are powerful words plainly setting our responsibility before us. Unless we are willing to extend ourselves to others, Satan will gain the advantage. Those are not my words; again they come from Paul. Unforgiveness, bitterness, and discouragement can overtake people who are already struggling and weak, and it is in just such moments that they can be "outsmarted by Satan" (2 Cor. 2:11).

The Listening Ear, the Hearing Heart

A comforting arm around the shoulder, a listening ear, and of utmost importance, a hearing heart—how necessary they all are to help ease the pain of another. Sometimes we just need to make it easy for someone to let down their defenses and cry. Tears are precious. Tears are so healing. One need never be ashamed of shedding them. Many were spilled in the Bible. Aren't we glad they were recorded!

At one point David, in great turmoil, cried out, "You have collected all my tears and preserved them in your bottle! You have recorded every one in your book" (Ps. 56:8).

Just as the blood of the saints, spilled through the years as they suffered for the cause of Christ, is precious to the Lord, so too are the tears we shed as we call out to God. They are not lost to him. God will reckon with those who have caused tears to come from his children's eyes. Prayer and tears, the psalmist told us, are good weapons for God's people as we face that which shakes us to the very roots of our faith.

Our sleepless nights, the tossings and the turnings, are known to our heavenly Father. In many places, we read of God saying, "I have seen thy tears." God doesn't hand out medals to those who do not weep. Weeping is a valid and normal emotion—even for men. God made men with a sensitive nature and the capacity to feel and experience emotions and grief. Remember, even "Jesus wept" (John 11:35 NIV). That happens to be the shortest verse in the Bible. But it conveys a large message.

The Bible assures us that "God is love" (John 4:8, 16). Life will be strong and rich and full of meaning in direct proportion to our willingness to accept God's love and appropriate all that he offers us into our daily lives. Moreover, as we release our capacity to love on the world, we will experience a peace and joy that is indescribable.

You've no doubt heard of the child who told his mother that he wanted a God with a face on. He was only expressing what humankind has always sought after—reality. He wanted a *someone*. Let us be walking love.

❧ 15 ❧

Man-Sized Problems
Require God-Sized Solutions

Faith demonstrates to the eye of the mind the reality of those things that cannot be discerned by the eye of the body. Faith is believing where we cannot see, trusting in Christ beyond the horizon, believing His goodness beyond our sight, trusting His word against the optic nerve.

J. Wallace Hamilton

A magazine article by an anonymous writer caught my attention at the time I found myself coming up out of the pit of despair. The writer was plagued by thoughts of wanting to kill himself. He admitted that Satan had him by the nose, leading him around, and life had become "a living hell," but death scared him because he had no real idea what lay beyond death.

It was this person's judgment that the mental anguish that induces suicidal thoughts becomes emotional illness. Mental pain, like physical pain, can become so unbearable that in desperation the person is driven to a remedy so drastic that he or she destroys all in trying to save part. In his anguish one fateful night, this man walked over to a window, stared out at the bright moon, and in a demanding voice shouted, "God, Jesus, or whoever you are! If you're really out there, if you're real and alive, if you can save me, you'd better do it in the next five minutes or forget about it!" He dropped to his knees and started to cry as he thought of the terrible things he'd done in his life and felt the urge to confess them, seeking forgiveness.

He remembered an exhilarating feeling settling over him, like he was being covered with a blanket of love. After years of wandering, ignoring, guessing, doubting, and playing games, just that quick he knew God was alive. He had gone down weak; now he got up strong with joy and hope. Talk about a miraculous, almost instantaneous answer to prayer! That certainly doesn't always happen, but thankfully, it did for this man. Obviously, God wasn't ready for this man to depart this earth.

He got out his Bible, and for the next few days, God began to reveal things to him that had long escaped his notice. He discovered Romans 10:17, which says faith comes by hearing, and hearing by the Word of God. He knew he was on the right track as God began guiding him into particular passages in the Bible. Providentially, he stopped at Psalm 40 and read, "I waited patiently for God to help me; then he listened and heard my cry. He lifted me out of the pit of despair, out from the bog and the mire, and set my feet on a hard, firm path and steadied me as I walked along. He has given me a new song to sing, of praises to our God" (vv. 1–3).

Of course, this arrested my attention, for this is how God broke through to me after I came to my senses. It was the same psalm, one of many into which I had retreated. The writer of the article thanked God for revealing to him through his Word the depths of his love and concern for him. "A few days before I had almost taken my life, with Satan standing there ready to yank me into eternity with him—a Christless eternity—when the Lord intervened and pulled me back to safety."

The man concluded the telling of his experience by stating: "I don't know exactly why God saved me from myself . . . but He did, and I'm mighty thankful. Man-sized problems require God-sized solutions. Go to the top for help."[1]

Stepping into Light

Why is the light of faith so often dim? I came across J. Wallace Hamilton's definition of faith early in my deepening walk with God, and I've never forgotten it: "Faith is believing where we cannot see, trusting in Christ beyond the horizon, believing His goodness beyond our sight, trusting His word against the optic nerve." Hamilton used to say, "If you want to believe, you have to stand where the light is shining."[2]

We must move out from the shadows, whatever that means in our individual experience. Perhaps for some it means venturing out where there are others who have found the light and exposing ourselves with some measure of regularity to the contagion of other people's faith. It means that one does not absent himself or herself from fellowshipping with other believers.

We have a biblical example of someone who wasn't with his fellow believers that night in the upper room when Jesus suddenly appeared in their midst after his crucifixion and resurrection. The disciples had assembled behind locked doors, in fear of the Jewish leaders, and now here was Jesus showing them his hands and side. Their joy was great, indescribable as they saw their Lord!

> One of the disciples, Thomas, "The Twin," was not there at the time with the others. When they kept telling him, "We have seen the Lord," he replied, "I won't believe it unless I see the nail wounds in his hands—and put my fingers into them—and place my hand into his side."
>
> Eight days later the disciples were together again, and this time Thomas was with them. The doors were locked; but suddenly, as before, Jesus was standing among them and greeting them. Then he said to Thomas, "Put your finger into my hands. Put your hand into my side. *Don't be faithless any longer. Believe!*"

John 20:24–27, italics added

How Does a Person Move from Unbelief to Faith?

What was Thomas's response? Immediate belief. "My Lord and my God!" (v. 28). Up until that moment, Thomas had been brooding in lonely solitude, burying his despair in feelings of hopelessness. He was gripped by the obsession that he could not possibly believe these wild stories about Jesus being alive and that he had appeared to the disciples. No, he couldn't—wouldn't—believe until he could see it for himself. He thought he had to see to believe.

Hamilton put it like this: "More than half the world is Thomas, afraid to believe. Half of every human heart is Thomas. . . . A man is at fault in his unbelief when, like Thomas, he stands in his own light; when he won't come where the light is; or when he won't expose his mind to the light. Look at him—this chronic doubter . . . Thomas, the man who missed the moment missed the Lord. Thomas lived for a week in the shadows of dark despondency, because he wasn't in the place where he was most likely to meet the Lord."[3]

What was Jesus's response to Thomas? "You believe because you have seen me. But blessed are those who haven't seen me and believe anyway" (v. 29).

We move from unbelief to belief, from faithlessness to faith, when we step from the shadows to the light and when we open our hearts to Christ.

That's what the anonymous writer of the article I quoted did. He had some knowledge of the Bible—one might call it a Sunday-school acquaintance with Bible stories and some Scripture—and on that fateful night when he reached the point where his mental pain was unbearable, he cried out to God. And that's all we have to do. The loving heavenly Father is always longing for his wayward children to cry and reach out to him. The Bible assures us this is true. For instance, in Psalm 139:7 we are told, "I can *never* be lost to your Spirit! I can *never* get away from my God."

As I did at the outset of this book, I urge you to turn to the Psalms, easy reading, comforting thoughts that seem to mirror our own. I remember finding Psalm 143, where it says, "I reach out for you. I thirst for you as parched land thirsts for rain. Come quickly, Lord, and answer me, for my depression deepens; don't turn away from me or I shall die. . . . Show me where to walk, for my prayer is sincere" (vv. 6–8).

When we walk near the shadow of death, as we do when we attempt suicide or even think about it, how much we need the help and hope that God provides, and he does this through passages like this in the Bible and as we seek him in prayer. We must keep our focus on God and indeed go to the top for help. Our man-sized problems do require God-sized solutions.

Doubting Thomas Has His Contemporaries Today

There are those today who are not unlike Thomas before that encounter with the risen Christ. They cheat themselves by reacting negatively in unbelief to emotional doubts that cloud the horizon. They insist on facts regarding this thing called faith and belief, when in many other matters they believe what they can't see, feel, or touch. Such insistence corrodes thinking.

For instance, the world, scientists say, is made of atoms. What do they mean, atoms? Show us some; let us see an atom. We don't see atoms, but we believe they exist. We believe in what we can't see. Men who couldn't see an atom split it.

We can't see electricity, energy, gravity, or the invisible link between cause and effect. How many things we accept and believe with confidence that we can't see at all. Have you ever seen an idea, felt a truth, or put your finger on a thought? The whole world of the mind, almost everything that is basic in personality—all of it is invisible to our eyes just as God is invisible.

Thomas thought he could at least trust his senses; what he could see and touch, he could believe. In his story, we see how deceptive the senses can be, and how little they grasp, and how much insight it takes to get back out of the way things appear to the way they actually are. Our senses can fool us, even in small things. Our eyes tell us the world is flat, but we know it isn't. They tell us that the sun rises, but we know it doesn't. They tell us the sky is blue, but the color is an optical illusion. You can't trust your senses. They don't tell you the whole truth about anything.

These illustrations from J. Wallace Hamilton colored my own perception of faith and belief. He provided the illustration of a ship sailing out to sea, and there, on what we call the horizon, it disappears. The horizon isn't real; it's only the limit of our vision, the place beyond which our sight cannot go. If we could see a little farther, we would know the truth—that the ship is just as big and just as real as when it left the harbor.

"Well, that is our faith. We believe what we cannot see. We trust in Christ beyond the horizon. We believe His goodness, beyond our sight. We trust His word against the optic nerve."[4]

The apostle Paul said, "The things which are seen are temporal; but the things which are not seen are eternal" (2 Cor. 4:18 KJV). His answer to the person who is filled with doubts and despairing of life is this: "So we do not look at what we can see right now, the troubles all around us, but we look forward to the joys in heaven which we have not yet seen. The troubles will soon be over, but the joys to come will last forever" (2 Cor. 4:18).

My prayer as I conclude this book is that if you have not experienced what has been shown in this chapter, that you too will go to the top for help and move from faithlessness to faith.

Appendix A

Resources for Suicide Prevention

If you or someone you know is suicidal, please contact a mental health professional or call (800) SUICIDE.

American Association of Suicidology

4201 Connecticut Ave. NW, Suite 408
Washington, DC 20008
(202) 237-2280
info@suicidology.org
www.suicidology.org

National Center for Injury Prevention and Control (NCIPC)

www.cdc/gov/ncipc/wisqars/default.htm (run by the
Centers for Disease Control and Prevention [CDC],
the National Institute of Mental Health [NIMH])
www.nimb.nih.gov/research/suicide.htm

National Organization for People of Color against Suicide (NOPCAS)

www.nopcas.com

The National Alliance for the Mentally Ill (NAMI)

1901 North Fort Myer Drive, Suite 500
Arlington, Virginia 22209
(703) 524-7600
(800) 950-NAMI

National Strategy for Suicide Prevention

www.mentalhealth.org/suicideprevention/index.htm

This is a collaborative effort between the Substance
Abuse and Mental Health Services Administration, the
Centers for Disease Control and Prevention, the National
Institutes of Health, and the Health Resources and Services
Administration. This site has links to various agencies with
resources for suicide prevention. The Surgeon General's
Call to Action to Prevent Suicide (1999) is available on
this site.

Schizophrenia

For detailed information about schizophrenia, in particular, write and ask for the research paper "Schizophrenia: Questions and Answers": DHHS Publication No. (ADM) 86-1457, Public Inquiries Branch, National Institute of Mental Health, Room 15C-05, 5600 Fishers Lane, Rockville, MD 20857. www.psy.med.rug.nl/0031.

Suicide Awareness Voices of Education (SAVE)

7317 Cahill Road, Suite 207
Minneapolis, MN 55439-0507
(952) 946-7998
Toll free: (888) 511-SAVE
www.save.org
save@winternet.com

Organizations That Focus on Depression

Phone these organizations to receive updated literature on depression.

American Psychiatric Association—(888) 267-5400
Campaign on Clinical Depression—(800) 228-1114
DEPRESSION/Awareness, Recognition, Treatment (D/ART) Program—(800) 421-4211
National Alliance for the Mentally Ill (NAMI)—(800) 950-NAMI or (800) 950-6264 (NAMI is a nonprofit organization that advocates for research and services in response to major illnesses that affect the brain.)

179

National Depressive and Manic-Depressive Association—
(800) 82 NDMDA
National Mental Health Association—(800) 969-NMHA

Christian Professional Counseling Organizations

Many of these organizations have referral information
databases.

American Association of Christian Counselors (AACC)

(800) 520-2268
www.aacc.net

Dr. Archibald Hart, who has written a number of fine
books on the subject of depression and mental health concerns, is the executive editor for this organization.

Christian Association for Psychological Studies

(800) 629-2277
www.capsintl@compuvision.net

North American Association of Christians in Social Work

(888) 426-4712
www.nacsw.org

Bent Tree Counseling Center (Dallas, TX)

(972) 248-7402

New Hope Crisis Counseling Center

(714) NEW-HOPE (639-4673)
www.newhopenow.org
12141 Lewis St.
Garden Grove, CA 92840

The New Hope Crisis Counseling Center was established by
Dr. Robert H. Schuller in 1968 as America's first twenty-four-
hour nationwide suicide prevention and telephone counseling
center sponsored by a church.

On June 1, 1997, Rev. Tim Milner and Dr. Bill Gaultiere
started NewHopeNow, featuring New Hope's free crisis counseling service in private chat rooms on the Internet, the first
service of its kind in the world. The heart of New Hope is its
team of over 350 volunteer counselors. Telephone counselors
serve in the Tower of Hope on the Crystal Cathedral campus
in Garden Grove, California. Internet counselors serve at the
Crystal Cathedral or from their home computers and live
in many states throughout America and in other countries
around the world.

Appendix B

Suicides Mentioned in the Bible

Some people mentioned in the Bible took their own lives. As explained earlier in this book, the word *suicide* itself isn't mentioned in Scripture, but the accounts of those who succeeded at ending their own lives is given here:

King Saul (1 Sam. 31:5). He fell on his sword.

Ahithophel (2 Sam. 17:23). He hanged himself.

Abimilech (Judg. 9:54). He asked his servant to kill him with his sword.

Zimri (1 Kings 16:18–19). He set the palace on fire and died in it.

Samson (Judg. 16:29–30). He pulled down the pillars on which the temple stood, saying, "Let me die with the Philistines."

Judas (Matt. 27:3–5). He hanged himself in remorse after his betrayal of Jesus.

Appendix C

Subtypes of Depression[1]

Unipolar depression: This is the most common form of depression, affecting over fifteen million Americans. "Unipolar" means there is no mania, just depressed mood, loss of ability to experience pleasure (anhedonia), feelings of worthlessness, guilt, etc.

Bipolar depression: This disorder alternates between severe depression and mania. In the depressed phase, the symptoms are the same as in unipolar depression, but in the manic phase, the person is expansive, excessively active, talkative, has grandiose ideas, and sleeps very little. About two million people in the United States are afflicted. It responds well to medications and mainly has genetic cause.

Atypical depression: So called because it involves chronic depression, excessive fatigue, oversleeping, overeating, etc. It is more difficult to treat and may require a combination of medications (called "polypharmacy").

Dysthymia: This is a fancy name for a low-grade depression that has lasted for more than two years and without a break for more than two months. Three to four percent are affected. While it was originally considered to be "neurotic," we now know that it is biological and can be treated the same way as unipolar depression.

Seasonal depression: For those living in the far north where there is insufficient sunlight for a large part of the year (more than five months), a "seasonal" depression, presumably caused by an excess of melatonin (a sleep hormone that is released in the brain with darkness), can set in. It is treated in "light rooms" where patients sit in rooms with bright lights similar to sunlight for several hours a day. Some homes in northern climates are now being equipped with such "sunrooms."

Psychotic depression: This is the severest of the depressions because it is accompanied by delusions or hallucinations. It requires immediate psychiatric care. About 15 percent of people with unipolar or bipolar depressions are affected.

Postpartum and other hormonal depressions: About 10 percent of new mothers experience depression, as do many women when they reach menopause. The problem is the dramatic drop in estrogen levels, and this requires medical treatment.

Appendix D

Recommended Reading

Anderson, Neil T. *The Bondage Breaker*. Eugene, OR: Harvest House, 2000.

Hart, Archibald D. *Unmasking Male Depression*. Nashville: Word, 2001.

Hart, Archibald D., and Catherine Hart Weber. *Unveiling Depression in Women*. Grand Rapids: Revell, 2002.

Hsu, Albert Y., *Grieving a Suicide*. Downer's Grove, IL: Intervarsity Press.

McFarland, Judy Lindberg. *Aging without Growing Old*. Lake Mary, FL: Siloam Press, 2003.

Moore, Pam Rosewell. *Finding Your Way through Depression*. Grand Rapids: Revell, 2005.

This is not intended as a comprehensive list of recommended reading material on the subject of suicide and depression. These are books that have helped me in the revision of this book, which is now into its third edition. Some resources listed are no longer in print, but the material is factually correct and has proved very helpful.

Notes

Introduction

1. The Surgeon General's Call to Action to Prevent Suicide, 1999 report, "At a Glance: Suicide Among Special Populations," provided by the Centers for Disease Control and Prevention.

Chapter 1 An Eclipse in My Soul

1. At one time Norman Farberow, Ph.D., was codirector of the Los Angeles Suicide Prevention Center. He was quoted in *Los Angeles Times Home Magazine*, June 2, 1974, which came to my attention at a time when I needed to read this.

2. Charles R. Swindoll, *The Mystery of God's Will* (Nashville: Thomas Nelson, 1999), 148.

Chapter 2 Could Something Be Missing?

1. Earl A. Grollman, *Suicide* (Boston: Beacon, 1973), 93.

2. Ibid., 23.

3. Duane Pederson, P.O. Box 1949, Hollywood, CA 90078-1949.

4. Dr. Maurice Rawlings, *Beyond Death's Door* (Nashville: Thomas Nelson, 1978), 19.

5. Ibid., 20.

6. A. W. Tozer, *The Knowledge of the Holy* (New York: Harper & Brothers, 1961), 47.

7. Wilma Stanchfield, with Helen Kooiman Hosier. *Struck by Lightning, Then by Love* (Nashville: Thomas Nelson, 1979), 167.

8. Tozer, *The Knowledge of the Holy*, 47–48.

Chapter 3 Nancy and Failed Suicide Attempts

1. Archibald D. Hart, *Unmasking Male Depression* (Nashville: Word, 2001), 91–92.
2. Elisabeth Elliot, *Shadow of the Almighty* (New York: Harper and Row, 1985), 77.

Chapter 5 Be Aware of Suicidal Gesturing

1. Paul W. Pretzel, *Understanding and Counseling the Suicidal Person* (Nashville: Abingdon Press, 1972), 45–46.
2. Brenda Rabkin, *Growing Up Dead* (Nashville: Abingdon, 1978), 127–29.
3. Ibid., 107.
4. Ibid., 123–24.
5. Ibid., 157.
6. Dr. Karl Menninger, *Man Against Himself* (New York: Harcourt, Brace, 1938).
7. *Christianity Today*, July 2000.
8. Pam Rosewell Moore, *Finding Your Way through Depression* (Grand Rapids: Revell, 2005), 25.
9. Hart, *Unmasking Male Depression*, 5.

Chapter 6 Women and Suicide

1. Lewis B. Smedes, "Is Suicide Unforgivable?" *Christianity Today*, July 10, 2000, 61.
2. Cimi Starr and Sherri Steiner, "Why Women Are Committing Suicide," *McCalls*, January 1976, 47.
3. Grollman, *Suicide*, 47.
4. Hart, *Unmasking Male Depression*, 13–14.
5. Ann Landers, "Prospective Suicides: Think of Those You'll Hurt," *Daily News Tribune*, June 8, 1974, A4. Used with permission.

Chapter 7 Men and Suicide

1. Frederick Buechner, *Telling Secrets* (San Francisco: Harper, 1991), 8.
2. Hart, *Unmasking Male Depression*, 16–17.
3. Ibid., 3.
4. Buechner, *Telling Secrets*, 7–9.
5. Ibid., 21–22.
6. Ibid., 34.
7. Ibid., 30.
8. Ibid., 33.
9. A. Alvarez, *The Savage God: A Study of Suicide* (New York: Random House, 1972).

10. Ronald Pollitt and Virginia Wiltse, *Helen Steiner Rice, Ambassador of Sunshine* (Grand Rapids: Revell, 1994).

11. Richard Cohen, "A Farmer's Suicide Raises a Question of Hypocrisy," *San Jose Mercury News*, December 18, 1985, 10C. The name of the farmer has not been included in my reporting of this article to protect family members and others in that Iowa community.

12. Ibid.

13. Ibid.

14. "Drugs and Suicide—a Problem on Both Sides of the Atlantic," *Psychology Today*, September 1973, 6.

15. J. B. Phillips, *The Price of Success, An Autobiography* (Wheaton, IL: Harold Shaw, 1984), 197.

16. Ibid., 200–1.

17. Ibid.

18. "Suicide by Auto," *Time*, July 11, 1977, 62.

Chapter 8 By Any Name, It's Tragic

1. Alvarez, *The Savage God.*

2. "Esthetics of Suicide," *Newsweek*, January 9, 1961, 25.

3. Nora Gallagher, "Why People Kill Themselves," *Today's Health*, February 1976, 50.

4. The Surgeon General's Call to Action to Prevent Suicide, 1999 report, "At a Glance: Suicide Among Special Populations," provided by the Centers for Disease Control and Prevention.

5. Ibid.

6. "Proud Indian ends hopelessness in suicide," *Denver Post*, February 9, 1986.

Chapter 9 Sad, Young, and Wanting to Die

1. Diane Eble, "Too Young to Die," *Christianity Today*, March 20, 1987, 21–22.

2. *Family Learning*, September/October 1984, 9. My research has spanned more than twenty years, and for the most part, the factual nature of these studies does not change. Statistics change, but the basic determinations of such information remain solid.

3. Hart, *Unmasking Male Depression*, 50.

4. Information gathered from the National Center for Injury Prevention and Control (NCIPC) website (www.cdc.gov/ncipc/wisqars/default.htm), a division of the Centers for Disease Control and Prevention (CDC), and the Morbidity and Mortality Weekly Reports (May 21, 2004, 53 [SS-2]; June 11, 2004, 53 (4), pp. 471–74).

Notes

Chapter 10 Depression and Suicide among the Older Population

1. Sherwood Eliot Wirt, *I Don't Know What Old Is, but Old Is Older than Me* (Nashville: Thomas Nelson, 1992), xv.

2. Ibid., 4.

3. Ibid., 1

4. Statistical information from the American Association of Suicidology, gathered from the National Center for Injury Prevention and Control (NCIPC) website (www.cdc.gov/ncipc/wisqars/default.htm) run by the Centers for Disease Control and Prevention (CDC). Information from 2002 latest available data.

5. Information gleaned from a fact sheet prepared by Suicide Awareness Voices of Education (SAVE), 7317 Cahill Road, Suite 207, Minneapolis, Minnesota 55439-0507. This is an organization dedicated to educating the public about suicide prevention. www.save.org.

6. Paul Tournier, *Learn to Grow Old* (New York: Harper & Row, 1972), 104–5.

7. Suicide Awareness Voice of Education, www.save.org.

8. Vance Havner, *Three Score and Ten* (Grand Rapids: Revell, 1973), 125–26.

9. Charles R. Swindoll, *Strengthening Your Grip* (Nashville: Word, 1982), 130–31.

10. Ibid., 132.

11. "Good Death?" *Time*, March 10, 1975, 83.

12. Wirt, *I Don't Know What Old Is, but Old Is Older than Me*, 8–9.

Chapter 11 Biblical People Who Expressed the Death Wish

1. J. Vernon McGee, *Through the Bible with J. Vernon McGee*, vol. 3 (Nashville: Thomas Nelson, 1982), 752.

Chapter 12 A Savage Enemy

1. Statements culled from the Release of the Mental Health Report, Washington, DC, December 13, 1999, provided by David Satcher, M.D., Ph.D., Assistant Secretary for Health and Surgeon General Office of Public Health and Science.

2. E. Fuller Torrey, *Surviving Schizophrenia: A Family Manual* (New York: Harper & Row, 1983).

3. There was a period of time in our nation's history when the mentally ill were placed in custodial care facilities, many of them "warehoused," as it were, in large, often dismal mental hospitals. Some of those still exist, but much of that has changed, and the trend, especially since a change in federal policy in 1971, has been away from such custodial care in mental hospitals, and as many patients as possible are being returned to their families and to their communities where they theoretically are encouraged to lead normal lives helped and sustained by medication and supervision. The reality is that this doesn't always happen, because many families simply will not take these individuals back in. Others just can't

189

cope with the often strange behavior and other problems associated with mental illness. So we have a terrible problem in the country because of these mentally ill who simply are not receiving the help they need.

4. Crystal Blyler, Ph.D., "New Hope for Coping with Schizophrenia," in *The Journal of NAMI California*, 11, no. 1:72–73.

5. Heather Barr, "We Have a New Community Mental Health System—It's Called Jail," *Journal of NAMI California*, 11, no. 3:24.

6. "Motherhood and Murder," and "The Baby Blues and Beyond," *Newsweek*, July 2, 2001.

7. Neil T. Anderson, *The Bondage Breaker* (Eugene, OR: Harvest House, 1993), 111.

8. Blyler, "New Hope for Coping with Schizophrenia."

9. Ibid.

10. Anderson, *The Bondage Breaker*, 20.

11. Chris Amenson, Ph.D., "Recovery for Families," *The Journal of NAMI California*, 11, no 1:68–70.

Chapter 13 The Role of Gatekeepers

1. Marshall Berges, "The Norman Farberows," *Los Angeles Times Home Magazine*, June 2, 1974, 46.

2. Thomas D. Kennedy, "Suicide and the Silence of Scripture," *Christianity Today*, March 20, 1987, 23.

3. Lewis B. Smedes, "Good Question, Is Suicide Unforgivable?" *Christianity Today*, July 19, 2000, 61.

4. Ibid.

5. Martin De Haan, "Been Thinking About a Heartache," *Times of Discovery*, October 2000.

Chapter 15 Man-Sized Problems Require God-Sized Solutions

1. Anonymous, "Go to the Top for Help," *These Times*, November 1972, 13–15.

2. J. Wallace Hamilton, *What About Tomorrow?* (Old Tappan, NJ: Revell, 1972), 59.

3. Ibid.

4. Ibid.

Appendix C   Subtypes of Depression

1. All descriptions in this appendix are quoted from Hart, *Unmasking Male Depression*, 24. Used with permission.

Helen Kooiman Hosier is well known in the field of Christian communications both as a writer and as a speaker. This bookstore owner turned author has more than sixty titles to her credit, including *Suddenly Unemployed*; *Living the Lois Legacy: Passing on a Lasting Faith to Your Grandchildren*; *100 Christian Women Who Changed the Twentieth Century*; *Beyond the Norm*; *Jonathan Edwards: The Great Awakener*; *William and Catherine Booth: Founders of the Salvation Army*; *Footprints: The True Story Behind the Poem*; *Living Cameos*; *Cameos: Women Fashioned by God*; and others. She conveys biblical principles with conviction and depth of understanding born out of her life experiences. She lives in Flower Mound, Texas.